First World War
and Army of Occupation
War Diary
France, Belgium and Germany

3 CAVALRY DIVISION
Headquarters, Branches and Services
Royal Army Ordnance Corps
Assistant Director Ordnance Services
2 September 1914 - 27 February 1919

WO95/1145/2

The Naval & Military Press Ltd
www.nmarchive.com
Published in association with The National Archives

Published by

The Naval & Military Press Ltd

Unit 10 Ridgewood Industrial Park,

Uckfield, East Sussex,

TN22 5QE England

Tel: +44 (0) 1825 749494

www.naval-military-press.com

www.nmarchive.com

This diary has been reprinted in facsimile from the original. Any imperfections are inevitably reproduced and the quality may fall short of modern type and cartographic standards.

© **Crown Copyright**
Images reproduced by permission of The National Archives, London, England, 2015.

Contents

Document type	Place/Title	Date From	Date To
Heading	WO95/1145/2		
Heading	1914-1919 3rd Cavalry Division Asst Dir. Ord. Services Sep 1914-Feb 1919		
Heading	D.A.D.O.S. 3rd Cavalry Division Sep-Dec 1914 to Feb 1919		
War Diary	War Office.	02/09/1914	02/09/1914
War Diary	At Patsmonth	03/09/1914	05/10/1914
War Diary	Ludgershall	06/10/1914	07/10/1914
War Diary	Ostend	08/10/1914	09/10/1914
War Diary	Bruges.	10/10/1914	10/10/1914
War Diary	Ootscamp.	11/10/1914	11/10/1914
War Diary	Thourout.	12/10/1914	13/10/1914
War Diary	Chateau Iseghem.	14/10/1914	20/10/1914
War Diary	St Jean.	21/10/1914	21/10/1914
War Diary	Voormezeele.	22/10/1914	31/10/1914
War Diary	Ypres	01/11/1914	19/11/1914
War Diary	Hazebrouck	20/11/1914	13/12/1914
War Diary	St Jans Capel	14/12/1914	15/12/1914
War Diary	Hazebrouck	16/12/1914	27/12/1914
Heading	D A.D.O.S. Jan to Dec 1915. (Oct. Missing)		
War Diary	Hazebrouck	28/12/1915	24/05/1916
War Diary	Renescure	26/05/1915	10/07/1915
War Diary	Heuringhem.	12/07/1915	31/07/1915
Heading	War Diary of D.A.D.O.S. 3rd Cav. Div. Period 2 September 1914 To 31 July 1915 Appendix I		
Miscellaneous	Indent For Stores, Clothing And Necessaries.	25/07/1915	25/07/1915
Heading	C3/3577		
Miscellaneous	Appendix 1 to War Diary		
Miscellaneous	Caps Service Dress. Summary of Indents for Bulk Issues.	19/07/1915	19/07/1915
Miscellaneous	Y		
Miscellaneous	War Diary. Appendix I Sheet 2	01/07/1915	01/07/1915
Heading	Major A.F.N. Barron. R.A. 2nd: Ord Dept DADOS 3rd Cavalry. Division From 1.8.15 To 31.8.15		
War Diary	Heuringhem	01/08/1915	04/08/1915
War Diary	Fauquemberge	05/08/1915	14/08/1915
Heading	Major A.F.N. Barron. R.A. 2nd Ord Dept. DADOS. 3rd Cavalry Division From 1.9.15 To 30.9.15		
War Diary	Fauquemberge	06/09/1915	10/09/1915
War Diary	Westrehem	21/09/1915	22/09/1915
War Diary	Laboussiere	24/09/1915	29/09/1915
War Diary	Fruges	05/11/1915	31/12/1915
Heading	War Diary of D.A.D.O.S. 3rd Cavalry Division Jan-Dec 1915 (Oct. Missing)		
War Diary	Fruges	01/01/1915	25/06/1915
War Diary	Domart	26/06/1915	26/06/1915
War Diary	La Neuville	27/06/1915	04/07/1915
War Diary	Hallencourt	05/07/1915	08/07/1915
War Diary	Daours	09/07/1915	31/07/1915
War Diary	Le Quesnoy	01/08/1915	01/08/1915

War Diary	Yvrench	02/08/1915	03/08/1915
War Diary	Leigescourt	04/08/1915	04/08/1915
War Diary	Fruges	05/08/1915	10/09/1915
War Diary	Maison Corthuie	11/09/1915	11/09/1915
War Diary	Belloy Sur Somme	12/09/1915	14/09/1915
War Diary	Daours	15/09/1915	30/09/1915
Heading	D.A.G. 3rd Echelon 42/8		
War Diary	Brevillers	01/10/1916	21/10/1916
War Diary	La Housoie	22/10/1916	31/12/1916
War Diary	Zailly	01/01/1917	04/01/1917
War Diary	Tupeid	05/01/1917	04/04/1917
War Diary	Maresquel	05/04/1917	06/04/1917
War Diary	Monihel	07/04/1917	07/04/1917
War Diary	Gouy En Artois	08/04/1917	08/04/1917
War Diary	Duisans	09/04/1917	11/04/1917
War Diary	Gouy En Artois	12/04/1917	16/04/1917
War Diary	Wavans	16/04/1917	19/04/1917
War Diary	Leigescourt	20/04/1917	12/05/1917
War Diary	Wavans	13/05/1917	13/05/1917
War Diary	Talmas	14/05/1917	14/05/1917
War Diary	Guerrieu	15/05/1917	16/05/1917
War Diary	La Motte	17/05/1917	18/05/1917
War Diary	Flamicourt	19/05/1917	31/05/1917
Heading	G. G. & G. M. S. 3rd Cav Div		
War Diary	Flamicourt	01/07/1917	03/07/1917
War Diary	Treux	04/07/1917	04/07/1917
War Diary	Doullens	05/07/1917	05/07/1917
War Diary	Framecourt	06/07/1917	06/07/1917
War Diary	Pernes	07/07/1917	16/07/1917
War Diary	Busnes	16/07/1917	31/08/1917
Heading	A.A & Q.M.G. 3rd Cav Div My War Diary For September 1917.		
War Diary	Busnes	01/09/1917	31/09/1917
War Diary	Busnes	01/10/1917	01/10/1917
War Diary	Pernes	17/10/1917	17/10/1917
War Diary	Hours-Houry	22/10/1917	22/10/1917
War Diary	Domart	23/10/1917	24/10/1917
War Diary	Domart En Ponthieu.	01/11/1917	16/11/1917
War Diary	Suzanne	17/11/1917	23/11/1917
War Diary	Beauquesne	23/11/1917	29/11/1917
War Diary	Corbie	30/11/1917	20/12/1917
War Diary	Domart En Ponthieu	21/12/1917	31/01/1918
War Diary	Monchy La Gache	31/01/1918	31/01/1918
War Diary	Monchy La Gache	01/02/1918	13/03/1918
War Diary	Athies	13/03/1918	21/03/1918
War Diary	Varesnes	22/03/1918	22/03/1918
War Diary	Carlepont	23/03/1918	23/03/1918
War Diary	Choisy au Bac	26/03/1918	26/03/1918
War Diary	La Croix St Dour	27/03/1918	27/03/1918
War Diary	No Evilly	28/03/1918	31/03/1918
War Diary	Rivery	01/04/1918	11/04/1918
War Diary	Auni le Chatheam	12/04/1918	12/04/1918
War Diary	Pernes	13/04/1918	04/05/1918
War Diary	Wail	05/05/1918	05/05/1918
War Diary	Yvrench	06/05/1918	06/05/1918
War Diary	Contay	06/05/1918	17/05/1918

War Diary	Yzeux	17/05/1918	01/08/1918
War Diary	Pont de Meti	06/08/1918	06/08/1918
War Diary	Bois de Bovres	08/08/1918	08/08/1918
War Diary	Yzeux	15/08/1918	15/08/1918
War Diary	Foustaine L'Pealon	06/09/1918	06/09/1918
War Diary	Marieuse	26/09/1918	26/09/1918
War Diary	Clery	27/09/1918	27/09/1918
War Diary	Goeuilly	30/09/1918	01/10/1918
War Diary	Maretz	10/10/1918	10/10/1918
War Diary	Clary	11/10/1918	11/10/1918
War Diary	Bertry	12/10/1918	12/10/1918
War Diary	Hinnois Wood	13/10/1918	01/11/1918
War Diary	Sainyhim	07/11/1918	07/11/1918
War Diary	Fruges	12/11/1918	12/11/1918
War Diary	Barsilly	17/11/1918	17/11/1918
War Diary	?	18/11/1918	18/11/1918
War Diary	Waterloo	21/11/1918	21/11/1918
War Diary	Perwey	22/11/1918	01/12/1918
War Diary	Soheit Tinlot	16/12/1918	23/12/1918
War Diary	Nandrin	29/12/1918	28/02/1919
War Diary	Engis	09/02/1919	27/02/1919

Nixon
1145(2)

1914-1919
3RD CAVALRY DIVISION

ASST DIR. ORD. SERVICES

SEP 1914 - FEB 1919

D.A.D.O.S

3rd Cavalry Division

Sep - Dec 1914

to

Feb. 1919

Army Form C. 2118.

WAR DIARY
or
INTELLIGENCE SUMMARY
(Erase heading not required.)

Instructions regarding War Diaries and Intelligence Summaries are contained in F. S. Regs., Part II. and the Staff Manual respectively. Title pages will be prepared in manuscript.

Hour, Date, Place	Summary of Events and Information	Remarks and references to Appendices
1 pm 2nd September War Office.	Appointed D.A.D.O.S. 3rd Cavalry Division.	
5.30 pm.	Returned to Portsmouth.	
3rd September to 6 September at PORTSMOUTH	Engaged during this period in forming a Camp Depot in Rondas for at Portsmouth in which Ordnance Stores and Ammunition required for equipping the units of 3rd Cavalry Division were subsequently assembled. A separate Camp Depot together with separate staff was necessary since 5 Gun Wharf Depot was already overtaxed in fitting out 7th Division and Staff work the fitting out of Portsmouth area refused current work of Head Quarters Woolwich.— Following Staff was sent from Head Quarters Woolwich:— 1 Warrant Officer, Chief Clerk. 1 S.O.M.S. Ledgers. Receipts 2 Privates (Issue him) Ledger Clerks. 1 S.O.M.S. Stockholder 2 S.S. Sergt Foreman and 24 Rank and File Storemen	T.B.M.P.

WAR DIARY

INTELLIGENCE SUMMARY

(Erase heading not required.)

Army Form C. 2118.

Instructions regarding War Diaries and Intelligence Summaries are contained in F. S. Regs., Part II. and the Staff Manual respectively. Title pages will be prepared in manuscript.

Hour, Date, Place	Summary of Events and Information	Remarks and references to Appendices
7 September to 20 September AT PORTSMOUTH.	The work of assembling the necessary equipment proceeded very slowly owing to the fact that the 3rd Cavalry Division was of special Establishment and that new A.F. G. 1098 had to be brought out for nearly every unit. The War Establishment of Division was not received before 20th. Approximate provision of these likely to be required was made by aid of a Statement furnished by War Office, but this proved a very unreliable guide. During the period most of the staff originally put down to Woolwich left, being called up to form Nos. 6 and 8 Companies R.E. They were replaced by New Army men who did remarkably well, often a few days, but the utter lack of knowledge of all staff in subject of Harness & Saddlery was a serious handicap, to a Field Depot equipping a Cavalry Division. One T.J.S.	

Army Form C. 2118.

WAR DIARY
or
INTELLIGENCE SUMMARY

(Erase heading not required.)

Instructions regarding War Diaries and Intelligence Summaries are contained in F. S. Regs., Part II. and the Staff Manual respectively. Title pages will be prepared in manuscript.

Hour, Date, Place	Summary of Events and Information	Remarks and references to Appendices
7 September to 30 September at Portsmouth.	S.Q.M.S. and myself were the only people who understood Harness & Saddlery at all efficiently and our knowledge was lacking on many points. The lack of training the Officers and N.C.Os & men get as regards Saddlery & Harness generally in our Depots has frequently been brought to my notice and I was convinced that on mobilization we should suffer by it. At Portsmouth I had my fears realized, as during the whole time the Depot work was severely handicapped owing to this lack of knowledge. It is recommended for sake of future efficiency that Storemen should be instructed specially as regards saddlery & harness. They would then be able to put sets together and to identify straps etc. – Regulations lay down that N.C.O & men should be trained in all branches, but constant shortage of staff at most depots precludes this being done. T.M.	

Army Form C. 2118.

WAR DIARY
or
INTELLIGENCE SUMMARY
(Erase heading not required.)

Instructions regarding War Diaries and Intelligence Summaries are contained in F. S. Regs., Part II. and the Staff Manual respectively. Title pages will be prepared in manuscript.

Hour, Date, Place	Summary of Events and Information	Remarks and references to Appendices
21 September at Portsmouth	as to Ordnance Officer cannot spare the men for instruction. War Establishment of Division received, also several revised A.F.G. 1098. Proceeded at once to demand actual requirements for each unit in those cases where covert provision had not already been made.	
22 September to 2 October at Portsmouth	Stores arrived very slowly. Allotment of wagons impossible as this was in War Office hands. Equipping cistern wrote as fully as possible and informed them that balance of Equipment would be issued when delivered by Woolwich. On evening of 2nd October received telegram ordering 3rd Cavalry Division units to be equipped at once. Telegraphed to Woolwich to send down all Equipment due by Passenger Train. Staff worked all night by aid of Naphtha Flare lights. T.M.L.	

1247 W 3299 200,000 (E) 8/14 J.B.C. & A. Forms/C/2118/11.

WAR DIARY
or
INTELLIGENCE SUMMARY

(Erase heading not required.)

Army Form C. 2118.

Instructions regarding War Diaries and Intelligence Summaries are contained in F. S. Regs., Part II. and the Staff Manual respectively. Title pages will be prepared in manuscript.

Hour, Date, Place	Summary of Events and Information	Remarks and references to Appendices
3rd October Saturday at Portsmouth	Received several telephone instructions from May – General Sir John Stevens as to entraining of wagons. Busy all day in allotting wagons to units, seeing mine marked, loaded on railway trucks. Units began taking to draw balances of equipment due. Horses provided throughout night which fortunately was fine. Many articles however not available. TMH	
4th October Sunday at Portsmouth	Every endeavour made to meet wants of units. Special train from Woolwich with stores. Worked in depot till Monday 2 A.M. when I handed over charge to Lieut Smythe and went home and got my kit together. TMH	
5 October Monday	Joined Hqrs 3rd Cavalry Division at SALISBURY as ordered. Motored Windmill Hill Camp LUDGERSHALL TMH	

1247 W 3209 200,000 (E) 8/14 J.B.C. & A. Form/C.2118/11.

Army Form C. 2118.

WAR DIARY
or
INTELLIGENCE SUMMARY
(Erase heading not required.)

Instructions regarding War Diaries and Intelligence Summaries are contained in F. S. Regs., Part II. and the Staff Manual respectively. Title pages will be prepared in manuscript.

Hour, Date, Place	Summary of Events and Information	Remarks and references to Appendices
Tuesday 6th October LUDGERSHALL	Up at 4 a.m. Divisional H.Qrs. entrained at 6-30 a.m. H.Q. Equipment put together anyhow and a lot left behind. Telegraphed C.O. Tidworth to send out Officers I took after and take charge of articles left behind.	
Southampton 11.30 a.m.	Embarked in S.S. HONORIUS.	
Wednesday 7th October	Sailed 1.30 a.m.	
Thursday 8th October OSTEND.	Arrived and disembarked. Rebilleted in OSTEND. At 9 pm a report by D.D.M.S. 4th Army acquired 100 Blankets for wounded Marines who had that evening arrived from ANTWERP and were being looked after at Konvent by Colonial Ambulance Corps.	
9.30 a.m. Friday 9th October OSTEND	Rode to BRUGES. Officers & men of Naval Division retreating from ANTWERP arrived at BRUGES. Knew several and specially looked after Lt Col FARRHARSON who was much exhausted. Billeted at The ? Vice Consuls. T.O.M.L.	

WAR DIARY
or
INTELLIGENCE SUMMARY

(Erase heading not required.)

Army Form C. 2118.

Instructions regarding War Diaries and Intelligence Summaries are contained in F. S. Regs., Part.II. and the Staff Manual respectively. Title pages will be prepared in manuscript.

Hour, Date, Place	Summary of Events and Information	Remarks and references to Appendices
10am Saturday, 10 October BRUGES.	Rode to OOTSCAMP and stopped there for night.	
Sunday 11 October OOTSCAMP.	Motored OSTEND via Bruges. Made arrangements for emptying Majors F. series and kits of H.Q. staff left behind at OSTEND. Billet to be sent to Ordnance Transit Depot. Bought blankets for men of Mobile Veterinary Section & others who had come out deficient.	
8.30 p.m.	Left OSTEND and rejoined H.Q.² at THOUROUT.	
Monday. 12 October THOUROUT.	Rode to ROULERS & stopped there for night.	
Tuesday. 13 October.	Motored YPRES in afternoon. Found telephone wire cut and German momentarily expected. On return found H.Q.ᵗˢ had been moved to ISEGHEM. Billetted ches Baron Gilles de Pelichy at Chateau.	T.B.A.

Army Form C. 2118.

WAR DIARY
or
INTELLIGENCE SUMMARY

(Erase heading not required.)

Instructions regarding War Diaries and Intelligence Summaries are contained in F. S. Regs., Part II. and the Staff Manual respectively. Title pages will be prepared in manuscript.

Hour, Date, Place	Summary of Events and Information	Remarks and references to Appendices
3.30.A.M. 14 October. CHATEAU ISEGHEM.	Left hospital very early morn as enemy were reported to be advancing. Rode to YPRES and then to WYTSCHAETE during the night about 8. p.m. in dark. Action in progress all day. Billeted in empty house.	
Thursday 15 October	Remained at WYTSCHAETE.	
Friday 16 October.	Rode to ZONNEBEKE. Billeted in Baker's house.	
Saturday 17 October	Remained ZONNEBEKE. Busy all day with clerical work. Colonel Matthew D.D.O.S. sent me typed instructions on various points.	
Sunday 18 October.	At Zonnebeke. S.Q.M.S. Staples and Private Dodds Baker reported for duty.	
Monday 19 October.	Moved with intention of stopping at MOORSLEDE. Enemy too strong and result of engagement was we fell back to St JULIEN, where we billeted in Cottage.	
Tuesday 20 October.	Moved to ABEELE to give orders to AMMUNITION Park. Billeted St JEAN this night. Slept like last night in Boots. T.J.M.	

WAR DIARY
or
INTELLIGENCE SUMMARY

(Erase heading not required.)

Army Form C. 2118.

Instructions regarding War Diaries and Intelligence Summaries are contained in F. S. Regs., Part II. and the Staff Manual respectively. Title pages will be prepared in manuscript.

Hour, Date, Place	Summary of Events and Information	Remarks and references to Appendices
Wednesday 21 October ST JEAN.	WP at 5 a.m. Village shelled about 9 a.m. Motored to Bailleul which was supply railhead for the day. We were now in touch with General French's Army and Ordnance Depôts thereof. Previously one had not been in touch with this source of supply and it had been impossible to get Ordnance stores except by local purchase. Finding no Fores for Division at BAILLEUL Railhead motored to HAZEBROUCK which was DISNAUATION Railhead. Found Colonel Mathew inspecting there and spoke to him. He kindly gave me full information as to how system of supply of ORDNANCE Stores was to be worked. Rejoined HQrs in evening and slept at CHATEAU GUEUME VOORMEZEELE for night.	
THURSDAY 22 October. VOORMEZEELE.	7.30 a.m. left CHATEAU. Motored railhead POPERINGHE. Got a room at INN and did clerical work connected with Indents now being received from Units in larger Numbers. Rejoined HQrs in afternoon + went into Billets at ZILLEBEKE. T.K.A.F.

T.K.A.F.

WAR DIARY
INTELLIGENCE SUMMARY

(Erase heading not required.)

Army Form C. 2118.

Hour, Date, Place	Summary of Events and Information	Remarks and references to Appendices
FRIDAY 23 OCTOBER	AT ZILLEBEKE. Engaged in Clerical work all day. Drafted orders and instructions re drawing & returning Ordnance Stores. 7th Division heavily engaged at ZONNEBEKE	TWL
SATURDAY 24th October.	Heavy firing during night. Guards Brigade arrived 2 A.M. and 8½ p.m. road. Went forward at 9 A.M. hearing Germans had broken through our head Quarters was temporarily moved to ZILLEBEKE in evening. Returned to ZILLEBEKE in evening.	TWL
Sunday 25 October.	Shells began to fall in neighbourhood & proprietor of house left.	TWL
Monday 26 October.	Very heavy rain during night. Employed most of day writing out to farmers - orderly required for Remounts coming up.	TWL
TUESDAY 27 October.	Motored Railhead CAESTRE. Got blocked on return and did not get back till 9.30 p.m.	TWL

WAR DIARY
or
INTELLIGENCE SUMMARY

(Erase heading not required.)

Army Form C. 2118.

Instructions regarding War Diaries and Intelligence Summaries are contained in F. S. Regs., Part II. and the Staff Manual respectively. Title pages will be prepared in manuscript.

Hour, Date, Place	Summary of Events and Information	Remarks and references to Appendices
Wednesday 28 October	Motored Railhead HAZEBROUCK. Motor skidded into lorry and damaged to steering gear so had to car was out of action. Major Hill DADOS of Division gave me a lift back to YPRES from which place I picked up a 3rd Cav Div't Motor — got back to Head Quarters 7PM	
Thursday 29 October	Enemy attacked. Heavy gun firing all day. Seely owing to Bthorn attack.	7PM
Friday 30 October	Renewed heavy firing & enemy again advanced. Left 8.30 am. for Railhead EBBLINGHEM. Got blocked on way, roads terribly bad with mud & traffic. On return to ZILLEBEKE found H.Q. had left + windows of our Billet broken by concussion. Re-occupied Billet that night but slept in boots.	7PM
Saturday 31 October	Up at 5.30 a.m. Billet again perked at 8 AM. Major BURNE DA QMG wounded in foot. Had lucky	

WAR DIARY
or
INTELLIGENCE SUMMARY

(Erase heading not required.)

Army Form C. 2118.

Hour, Date, Place	Summary of Events and Information	Remarks and references to Appendices
	escapes myself as when motoring to/from Klein ZILLEBEKE shells fell just before and behind car. On return to HQ" found another couple of shells had just burst in, killing 6 Frenchmen, 4 of whom were officers and wounding dozens. Col. Davey A.A.& M.G. proceeded to EBBLINGHEM taking an officer who Baker when bone to YPRES on to way. Bn MM. whom I found HQ" at YPRES. (saved stores & 6. Cars B.M. ???. Lovely Day.	
Sunday 1 November. YPRES		
Monday 2 November. YPRES	Motored Roikhad EBBLINGHEM. Took 4 hours MM. getting there.	
Tuesday 3 November. YPRES	Hooge Road now shelled. 4 horses billet ridden our stores were dumped previous night and Private Babcock who was in charge had had lucky MM. escape.	

WAR DIARY or INTELLIGENCE SUMMARY

Army Form C. 2118.

Hour, Date, Place	Summary of Events and Information	Remarks and references to Appendices
Wednesday 4 November YPRES	Had F shift on Billet porter down stairs as it was getting too warm - house close to Hdqrs hold. Rode out to 6 E Cav Brigade. HOOGE Road under Gunfire. Heavy firing into YPRES this day. 3rd Dragoon Guards joined 1st Division them making 6 Cav. Bde now 3 Regt strong. THW	
THURSDAY 5 November YPRES	Motored STRAZEELE Railhead. Very seedy going to CWM. Disastrous fire occurred in retail 4 men of HQ 6 Cav [?] & 6th went burnt to death & severely burned. Probably due to smoking in a loft. THW	
FRIDAY 6 November YPRES	Motored STEENBECQUE. Took 6 hours getting here owing to unexpected Fondo. Heavy foggy night. STOPPED at HAZEBROUCK for night. THW	
Saturday 7 November YPRES	Motored STEENBECQUE. No stores. Returned YPRES. New Billet to HQ on outskirts of Town. My groom nearly killed by being kicked by my horse & knocked home senseless. THW	

WAR DIARY
or
INTELLIGENCE SUMMARY

(Erase heading not required.)

Army Form C. 2118.

Instructions regarding War Diaries and Intelligence Summaries are contained in F. S. Regs., Part II. and the Staff Manual respectively. Title pages will be prepared in manuscript.

Hour, Date, Place	Summary of Events and Information	Remarks and references to Appendices
Sunday 8 November YPRES.	Up at daylight and went straight off to STEENBECQUE Paillam stopping at STEENVORDE for Wash + breakfast. Prisoners journey up here were no stores. Roads very bad and congested as usual. Got back 4pm. YPRES in flames. Still holding on own trenches and all apparently going well. Following orders published in Pickets RO No 20 Para 3. Officers armed with Colts .45 Automatic Pistol for which ammunition is not available from Ordnance Department. Can of them will have them exchanged for Webley and Scott Revolvers on payment. TMH	
Monday 9 November YPRES.	Up at daylight. Motored STEENBECQUE via ABEELE. Breakfasted at Brun + Park at ABEELE. Got two lorry loads stores. TMH	
Tuesday 10 November YPRES	Commenced a busy down to STEENBECQUE. Roads very bad. Plenty of tries at Railhead. Got back after dark. Beety hurt head light - would not work. During last 2 miles had to shine my self - chauffeur sticking by walking along middle of road with oil lamp. Very late petting home. TMH	
Wednesday 11 November YPRES	Did office work all day. Very heavy shunting. 14 inch shell doing a good deal of damage to buildings. Windy + wet. TMH	

WAR DIARY
or
INTELLIGENCE SUMMARY

Army Form C. 2118.

(Erase heading not required.)

Hour, Date, Place	Summary of Events and Information	Remarks and references to Appendices
Thursday 12 November YPRES.	Motored STEENBECQUE - Tried to purchase Mess Carts locally without success. Did not get back before dark.	TW
Friday 13 November YPRES	Very wet. Following orders published this day. R.O. N° 24 para 3. Ordnance Stores. Provision and supply of Special Stores and articles in excess of the authorized scales of equipment) laid down in Mobilization Stor Tables will not be provided with by G of C. without approval having been previously obtained through G.H.Q. It is therefore necessary that O.C. Units requiring such stores should apply to put forward O'orders for approval of G.O.C. If approval by him to application is forwarded to G.H.Q for final decision of Q.M.G., and it is only when this decision is favourable that action can be taken by D.A.D.O.S and Indents passed to Base for supply. TW	

WAR DIARY
INTELLIGENCE SUMMARY

(Erase heading not required.)

Army Form C. 2118.

Hour, Date, Place	Summary of Events and Information	Remarks and references to Appendices
Saturday 14 November YPRES.	Met Colonel Mathew (?) D.D.O. at STEENBECQUE. Major STEPHEN, Captain Moore-Allen and myself represented to him our difficulties and he took note and promised that more lorries should be placed at our disposal, etc.	TML
Sunday 15 November YPRES.	Sleeting hard and very cold. Church service at 7 A.M. Occupied in clerical work during day.	TML
Monday 16 November YPRES.	Motored STEENBECQUE - got back before dark.	TML
Tuesday 17 November YPRES.	Wet day. Visited Brigades.	TML
Wednesday 18 November YPRES.	Motored STEENBECQUE. Withams appeared in R.O. Following order re Winter Clothing campaign. It is hoped that if we have another winter campaign the winter clothing will be available for issue earlier for men are badly in need of it. It is mostly today. R.O. 26. Para 1. Winter Clothing. The scale of winter clothing laid down in	

WAR DIARY
or
INTELLIGENCE SUMMARY

(Erase heading not required.)

Army Form C. 2118.

Instructions regarding War Diaries and Intelligence Summaries are contained in F. S. Regs., Part II. and the Staff Manual respectively. Title pages will be prepared in manuscript.

Hour, Date, Place	Summary of Events and Information	Remarks and references to Appendices
	Routine Order N° 12. para 15 dated 26/10/14 for the following articles is hereby cancelled viz: Shoes, Goats, Stockings British warm Coats, Mackintoshes, Gloves Gauntlets Sweaters and to following substituted. Units should so submit Indents Showing sizes for those articles on the New scale to D.A.D.O.S. without delay and issues will be made as supplies become available.	
	Description of Articles	Unit to which issued
	Coats, fur lined	Drivers of Motor Lorries & Cars & Horsed Transport Vehicles other than 1st Line.
	Coats B.W. lined khaki	M.S. not issued with Coats fur lined.
	Waistcoats fur	All dismounted services including cyclists (but not motor cyclists). (Not necessary except in Trenches. Too bulky & hot for cyclists. TMcy.)

WAR DIARY or INTELLIGENCE SUMMARY

Army Form C. 2118.

Hour, Date, Place	Summary of Events and Information	Remarks and references to Appendices
Wednesday 18 Nov YPRES.	Description of Articles — Scarves for which issued.	
	Jackets leather } Overalls leather }	All motor cyclists
	Coats B.W. } Caps Maudrivers }	Cyclists (not motor cyclists)
	Gloves leather wool lined } in M.T. Rfr. }	Motor car drivers, lorry drivers & motor cyclists. TMcC
Thursday 19 November.	Division returned to Transloic & moved back to HAZEBROUCK area. Divisional Head Quarters refused to move to LAMOTTE very busy saying that units did not know where to billets owing to refusing equipment. On arrival = afternoon at LAMOTTE and found billets, orders cancelling LAMOTTE as billeting area received. The same were required for Cavalry Corps Head Quarters. Went out and proceeded to HAZEBROUCK & then dark before billets could be found. TMcC	

Army Form C. 2118.

WAR DIARY
or
INTELLIGENCE SUMMARY

(Erase heading not required.)

Instructions regarding War Diaries and Intelligence Summaries are contained in F. S. Regs, Part II. and the Staff Manual respectively. Title pages will be prepared in manuscript.

Hour, Date, Place	Summary of Events and Information	Remarks and references to Appendices
Friday 20 November. HAZEBROUCK.	With approval of G.O.C. suggested a large thinned Carpenters shop at Back of Billet for use as a Distributing store. Wired to Base that Division had come back to refit and that I was prepared to receive unlimited quantities of Winter Clothing and equipment, large quantities of which were due. Weather cold and roads very slippery with ice. No frost nails or large mittens to meet the repeated applications of units.	THH
Saturday 21 November HAZEBROUCK.	Following notice appeared in Divisional Routine Orders of this date. The role of the Temporary Ordnance Depôt for issue of trousers, Frost nails, Button Winter clothing and other articles when we arriving in bulk for distribution to units is to form a Prefecture Hazebrouck close which is 20 mm to do so. Prefecture Hazebrouck close to H.Q of Division. Advice has been received that a supply of Frost nails, woven woollen vest, gloves, mufflers have been put on rail. It is hoped that some of these articles will commence on Monday.	THH

WAR DIARY
or
INTELLIGENCE SUMMARY

(Erase heading not required.)

Army Form C. 2118.

Hour, Date, Place	Summary of Events and Information	Remarks and references to Appendices
Sunday 23 November HAZEBROUCK	Large quantity of stores received Railhead. Very cold. Skating hard. My Carpenters shop which is a large building with 20 empty Carpenters benches and a boat central gangway was by 1 pm filled with toles & packages. Afternoon spent in treating beds & laying out in detail for units.	
Monday 24 November to Saturday 28 November	More stores received. Indents commence to pour in and to Division two frantically to be re-equipped entirely. Work for all is steadier inurwand and one day being same as another. Men proved & milk of having weekly only.	TWM
Sunday 29 November — Saturday 5 December	Daily routine: reveillé & visit to Railhead STEENBECQUE. Parade at 9 a.m. — Receipt and issue of stores during day. — Nightly Indents and correspondence till midnight. Horse Rugs approved for issue this week. On 2nd December 1st Division was inspected by H.M. The King. B Section 20 M Field Ambulance joined to Division. Truth ultimately received of Can. Field Ambulance I understand.	TWM

WAR DIARY
or
INTELLIGENCE SUMMARY

(Erase heading not required.)

Army Form C. 2118.

Hour, Date, Place	Summary of Events and Information	Remarks and references to Appendices
Sunday 6 December to Saturday 13 December. HAZEBROUCK	Daily visit to Railhead. Heavy consignments of stores, but quite insufficient to satisfy demands of units. Warm clothing coming up satisfactorily. 8th Signal Troop ordered to be formed. G. Battery R.H.A. joined Division. The 8th Cavalry Brigade will consist of Royal Horse Guards, 10th Hussars, Essex Yeomanry. Leave is being granted to officers and men to proceed to England. 8th Division left HAZEBROUCK for St JANS CAPPEL, a small village near BAILLEUL. Staff in vicinity of to proceed to scenes at St Vincent de Paul. Our office Numa was English.	TMB

Army Form C. 2118.

WAR DIARY
or
INTELLIGENCE SUMMARY

(Erase heading not required.)

Instructions regarding War Diaries and Intelligence Summaries are contained in F. S. Regs., Part II. and the Staff Manual respectively. Title pages will be prepared in manuscript.

Hour, Date, Place	Summary of Events and Information	Remarks and references to Appendices
14 & 15 December ST. JANS CAPEL	Very wet. Division standing by to move at short notice. Issue of Dandy Brushes approved and also hand allowance of Lanterns. Tent fleting increased.	
16 December. Tuesday HAZEBROUCK	Moved back again into same billets at HAZEBROUCK.	
17 December Wednesday	Ordinary Routine. Daily visit to STEENBECQUE Road.	
20 December Saturday.	Head Dresser Clippers Horses authorized at rate of 1/pr each Vet? officer & 2 for each Mobile Vet Section.	M.M.B.
21st December Sunday	Ordinary Routine. On 24th December went home	
24th December	to England on leave till 27th December	
25 – 27 December	On leave. L.T. Col. De Fer Nth Fd. Barry D.A. & QMG got orders for home on Xmas Day	M.M.B.

1247 W 3209 200,000 (E) 8/14 J.B.C. & A. Forms/C.2118/1.

DADOS

Jan to Dec. 1915

(oct missing)

Army Form C. 2118.

WAR DIARY
or
INTELLIGENCE SUMMARY
(Erase heading not required.)

Instructions regarding War Diaries and Intelligence Summaries are contained in F. S. Regs., Part II. and the Staff Manual respectively. Title pages will be prepared in manuscript.

Hour, Date, Place	Summary of Events and Information	Remarks and references to Appendices
Sunday 28 December to Saturday 2 January. HAZEBROUCK	Ordinary Routine. Incidents still very numerous. Great shortage of large sized Pantaloons. The material of the pantaloons supplied very inferior & shoddy and the Boots also very bad. Soles of latter often go out in water almost at once. The Field Service Boot very popular and a good boot. Only 40 pairs per Cavalry Regiment available for issue, however, North Writes this boot would be supplied to every Cavalry Soldier with a pair of Ordinary Boots & full lock on, & to carried onto saddle so to Bench do. W.M.	
Sunday 3 January to Saturday 9 January. in HAZEBROUCK	Ordinary Routine. Imported Transport of Division with O.C. D.S.C. found much adrift. Badly fitting Harness. Wheels not washed up. Broken reins. Deficient Whips. Equipment. Heavy indents received in consequence of this inspection. Several Civilian pattern wagons W. M.	

1247 W 3259 200,000 (E) 8/14 J.B.C. & A. Forms/C. 2118/11.

WAR DIARY
or
INTELLIGENCE SUMMARY

Army Form C. 2118.

Hour, Date, Place	Summary of Events and Information	Remarks and references to Appendices
10 January Sunday to 16 January Saturday at HAZEBROUCK	STEENBECQUE continues to be Railhead for Supplies. Ordinary routine. Stores coming up fairly satisfactorily. Difficulty that all horseshoes of correct size are used. A Sanitary Section has been added to the Division. Notified in Routine Orders that Ammunition Mules 13 & 18 pr. AF need worth returning, but can be broken up. This seems a pity as they will probably be a shortage of them at home before many months are over and they could easily be collected at Bases in this country for use when required. Horse shoe boxes also which must cost at least 30/- Lshillings each are not kept. TMR	

Army Form C. 2118.

WAR DIARY
or
INTELLIGENCE SUMMARY
(Erase heading not required.)

Instructions regarding War Diaries and Intelligence Summaries are contained in F. S. Regs., Part II. and the Staff Manual respectively. Title pages will be prepared in manuscript.

Hour, Date, Place	Summary of Events and Information	Remarks and references to Appendices
Sunday 17 January	Ordinary Routine. Nothing to record — Daily journeys to Poitterd. Distribution of Xmas in receipt	
Saturday 23 January. at HAZEBROUCK	Effected local purchase of 400 Dandy Brushes at ST. OMER at 1/- a piece —	TMW
Sunday 24 January.	Inspected Transport of Division again — Great improvement by many regiments, however, not good.	
Saturday 30 January HAZEBROUCK	Division ordered to send 3000 men to Trenches next week by Brig. Wired for extra Braziers etc.	TMW
31 January Sunday	On 1 February Colonel Stewart A.D.O.S Cavalry Corps joined up and became temporary member of B.	
6 February Saturday HAZEBROUCK	Mess — 3000 men entrained for Trenches on 3 February.	TMW

1247 W 3299 200,000 (E) 8/14 J.B.C. & A. Forms/C. 2118/11.

WAR DIARY or INTELLIGENCE SUMMARY

Army Form C. 2118.

Hour, Date, Place	Summary of Events and Information	Remarks and references to Appendices
7 February – 13 Feb'y HAZEBROUCK	On 10th February the Billets occupied by our Reserve Troops were shelled and 6 men of 1st Life Guards were killed and 7 wounded. Only what is termed A. Echelon Transport goes up to front with Ration parties. B Echelon – G.S. wagons, ammunition, kitchens and one man looks after 4 or 5 horses. When Trench party comes out of Trenches here as always every demands for hot equipment and necessaries Ordnance lorry goes up daily taking up only that actually required in Trenches, remainder is delivered at B Echelon H.Q. of unit. On 11 Feb'y I moved my office and Distribution Stn to another part of HAZEBROUCK in order to be partly with the rest of my Army, the town now being mainly occupied by 1st Army & 2nd Army Troops, only small portion of Indian & Cavalry Corps On 13 Feb'y our men were relieved in the Trenches	MWD

Army Form C. 2118.

WAR DIARY
or
INTELLIGENCE SUMMARY
(Erase heading not required.)

Instructions regarding War Diaries and Intelligence Summaries are contained in F. S. Regs., Part II. and the Staff Manual respectively. Title pages will be prepared in manuscript.

Hour, Date, Place	Summary of Events and Information	Remarks and references to Appendices
14 February — 20 February HAZEBROUCK.	Ordinary Routine. The way ptes are put up by Base is slowly but surely getting better day by day. New motor car received on 18 t. a closed in Daimler. Very top heavy but useful in this cold and wet weather. My old Motor car returned to Base with grave gun g inferior metal, over case hardened — a common fault with new Daimlers. T/WE	
21 February to 27 February HAZEBROUCK.	Nothing to chronicle. Wrote all proper lamps hurricane to to Lantern Tent polishing. Good lamps of local manufacture seem to be bought for life. 50. several fires have occurred in farms & hemes of all descrips to naked lights. The Candle lantern gives such a feeble illumination that un- protected candles in probably most in addition. Scale of lanterns should be increased for winter months. T/WE	

WAR DIARY
or
INTELLIGENCE SUMMARY

(Erase heading not required.)

Army Form C. 2118.

Hour, Date, Place	Summary of Events and Information	Remarks and references to Appendices
28 February to 6 March. HAZEBROUCK	Nothing to record.	TMcC
7 March to 13 March. HAZEBROUCK.	From 10th to 13th March the Division was standing by ready to move at very short notice in case it NEUVE CHAPELLE attack was a success.	TMcC
14 March to 20 March. HAZEBROUCK.	Battle of St. Eloi. Division standing by.	TMcC
21 March to 27 March. HAZEBROOK.	The 4 A.B. th R.H.A. during this week left for LOCRE and temporarily joined II Army. Equipment was continued to supplied by me, however, a lorry going out there as necessary.	TMcC

Army Form C. 2118.

WAR DIARY
or
INTELLIGENCE SUMMARY
(Erase heading not required.)

Instructions regarding War Diaries and Intelligence Summaries are contained in F. S. Regs., Part II. and the Staff Manual respectively. Title pages will be prepared in manuscript.

Hour, Date, Place	Summary of Events and Information	Remarks and references to Appendices
28 March to 3 April HAZEBROUCK	ORDINARY Routine — Nothing special to chronicle.	
4 April to 10 April HAZEBROUCK	Visited C Battery, all Returned. Spent some hours in afternoon of 7th in Observation Station watching to resulte of the Battery firing. On 10 April the new system of telegrams came into force, whereby Special Bulk Rate were used for an, Amsterdam day once a week. A great improvement.	
11 April – 17 April HAZEBROUCK	Frost cops. Traps & Wrenches & foot raids withdrawn this week.	
18 April – 24 April HAZEBROUCK	On 22nd Hadlts of 9th Indian Jorst employment of Gas. Divn & Echelons moved up to OUDERDOM, POPERINGHE, VLAMERTINGHE. Established an advanced general Ordnance Depot at POPERINGHE, some being in charge of Col Archdale Robert.	

Army Form C. 2118.

WAR DIARY
or
INTELLIGENCE SUMMARY
(Erase heading not required.)

Instructions regarding War Diaries and Intelligence Summaries are contained in F. S. Regs., Part II. and the Staff Manual respectively. Title pages will be prepared in manuscript.

Hour, Date, Place	Summary of Events and Information	Remarks and references to Appendices
18 April – 24 April (continued)	The lorry contained extra socks, blankets, gum boots etc for men in Trenches if required. Little was issued but kept was very useful and all stock was taken over by 3rd Can. Div. when they relieved our Division.	
25 April – 1 May. HAZEBROUCK.	Nothing to chronicle. Brisk deliveries of Ordnance stores were made to A Echelon by Motor lorries.	
2 May – 8 May. HAZEBROUCK	A Echelon returned to Poperinghe – 1 May. Major gen. C.J. BRIGGS C.B. assumed command of Division on 7 May. On 8 May 11th Co. was equipped.	
9 May –	A Echelon, 3000 rd. moved to Trenches again Billetted at VLAMERTINGHE.	
10 May.	Motored up with VERY PISTOLS. Shelling near our H.Q. some civilians have killed just part of pier there.	
12 May	Division took over line of Trenches HOOGE & POTIZE.	

Forms/C. 2118/11.

WAR DIARY or INTELLIGENCE SUMMARY

Army Form C. 2118.

Hour, Date, Place	Summary of Events and Information	Remarks and references to Appendices
13 May	7th Cavalry in Trenches before YPRES heavily shelled. Trenches too shallow and consequently men there shelled out. 6th Cavalry Brigade whose trenches were better, managed to hang on. Lost Trenches retaken at 2.30 pm by a brilliant and gallant counter attack by 8th Cav. Brigade. This fighting cost K. Division heavy loss. Over 90 officers killed and wounded, and over 1000 N.C.O. & men ditto. Out of 9 Colonels commanding Regiments 7 killed or wounded. VWL	
14 May	Despatched heavy indents for new equipment. 10 Vickers guns lost or rendered unserviceable and much other equipment.	VWL
15 May	Further requirements hourly reported.	
16 May	Advised that Base had despatched 7 Tons of equipment.	VWL

Army Form C. 2118.

WAR DIARY
or
INTELLIGENCE SUMMARY

(Erase heading not required.)

Instructions regarding War Diaries and Intelligence Summaries are contained in F. S. Regs., Part II. and the Staff Manual respectively. Title pages will be prepared in manuscript.

Hour, Date, Place	Summary of Events and Information	Remarks and references to Appendices
17 May – 22 May. HAZEBROUCK.	MICA windows of SMOKE HELMETS proving very unsatisfactory, and Routine Order prohibited their respirators must be carried a worn in rotation.	
23 May / HAZEBROUCK.	Packing up prior to moving billets.	
24 May	Moved to RENESCURE.	
26 May to 29 May RENESCURE.	On 28th Colonel Kenward A.D.O.S Cavalry Corps proceeded in search and looked for him. letter O.P.B. 1170 Arrived War Office have asked that final S.A.A. cases stating as follows: should not be sent to England, will you please therefore not that it is not necessary to extract them for return to Base.	
30 May to 5 June. RENESCURE.	Letters as follows. O.C. 696. dated 1.6.15. Reference your O.B.1170 please inform that no steps whatever are now to be taken to preserve to old Brass noted recoverable from fired .303 S.A.A. cases now fired. These fired cases all to be buried or otherwise to be collected at ammunition railheads with a view to local sale of French authorities officered. Reply issued [illegible] of letter was enforced. Outlined Routine orders accordingly.	

Army Form C. 2118.

WAR DIARY
or
INTELLIGENCE SUMMARY
(Erase heading not required.)

Instructions regarding War Diaries and Intelligence Summaries are contained in F. S. Regs., Part II. and the Staff Manual respectively. Title pages will be prepared in manuscript.

Hour, Date, Place	Summary of Events and Information	Remarks and references to Appendices
10 June, RENESCURE	Division resting at RENESCURE. Squadron Inspection the order of the day. Heavy demands for Equipment fall kinds to replace articles worn out & lost during to recent turn in Trenches.	
12 June, RENESCURE	STEENBECQUE — Wolseley Car, off front wheel come off through breaking of Stub axle, a common accident in these cars. Car went into ditch but otherwise no damage. Weather very fine except for thunderstorm.	WH
13 June to 19 June, RENESCURE	O.C. A.S.C. inspected Transport of units this week. Many vehicles in need of Repair & all want painting. The majority of G.S. limbered waggons are deficient of brakes. The MK I brake is stronger & more satisfactory than to MK II, through heavier.	WH

Army Form C. 2118.

WAR DIARY
or
INTELLIGENCE SUMMARY
(Erase heading not required.)

Instructions regarding War Diaries and Intelligence Summaries are contained in F. S. Regs., Part II. and the Staff Manual respectively. Title pages will be prepared in manuscript.

Hour, Date, Place	Summary of Events and Information	Remarks and references to Appendices
20 June to 26 June. RENESCURE	Mentioned in Despatches 23 June — The order directing troops not to collect and send fired S.A.A. cases to Railheads for transmission to Base was cancelled on 23rd June, after having been in existence three weeks — I was sure there was some error in the original order for to allow good brass to be wasted seemed bound to be wrong — Wallets for Cavalry Horses will now be sent up in the goatskins and will be a great convenience to troops — TMW	
27 June to 3 July RENESCURE	Nothing of spec'l General routine. Stores coming up very well. "System of Supply" working well. TMW	For full detailed description of present system of supply as worked in this Division see APPENDIX I. TMW
4 July to 10 July RENESCURE	Ditto — TMW	

WAR DIARY
or
INTELLIGENCE SUMMARY

(Erase heading not required.)

Army Form C. 2118.

Hour, Date, Place	Summary of Events and Information	Remarks and references to Appendices
12 July to 17 July. HEURINGHEM.	On 12th instant moved billets back to HEURINGHEM having main road clear for to new divisions coming through.	TMcL
18 July to 24 July. HEURINGHEM.	Ordinary Routine. This consisted of early visit to Railhead & superintendence of distribution of Bulk Issue at Distribution point. Returned to Chauffeurs diary shows following mileage— Monday 65 miles, Tuesday 90 miles, Wednesday 60 miles Thursday 65 miles, Friday 80 miles, Saturday 60 miles.	TMcL
25 July – 31 July.	Ordinary Routine. From 29 July acting as ADOS car G6 during temp absence on leave of Col Stewart AOD. On same day received orders to proceed to Boulogne to take up appointment of Ordnance Officer vice Major Clark of early date. Arranged to hand over to Major Barron who relieves me on 1 August. —— Finis ——	TMcL

WAR DIARY
of
D.A.D.O.S 3rd Cav. Div
Period 2 September 1914
to
31 July 1915

APPENDIX I

Army Form G. 994.

INDENT FOR STORES, CLOTHING AND NECESSARIES.

Indent No. ST42 Date 25/7/15

Corps 7th Signal Troop

To be sent to OC 7th Signal Troop

To arrive by As soon as posible 3rd Cav Divn

For A.O.D. use only.

ISSUE No.
C.313577
26/7/15

I certify that the following articles are actually required to complete to authorized scale:—
(a) As a first supply.
(b) To replace others lost through the exigencies of the campaign.
(c) To replace others rendered unserviceable through the exigencies of the campaign.

Signed _Muir Lieut_ Approved for issue. _T M Raby Major_

Commanding 7th Signal Troop AADOS 3rd Cav Divn

Articles Required.	Quantity.	For A.O.D. use.	Articles Required.	Quantity.	For A.O.D. use.
Pants Riding SD size 2	1 pr.		ob.		
Caps SD 6⅞ 16⁹/8.1.7	3		Copy		Bulk
Razors	6				
Braces	6 pr				from ARLS
Anklets Army Serv. L.	12			Bag	
Jacket S.D. size 2	1				Bulk
Knives Clasp	8				Special Item

C3/3577

Appendix I to War Diary

Details of System of Supply of Ordnance
Stores employed in 3rd Cavalry Division
on 1st July 1915 while Division is in
Stationary Billets.
   by Major Leahy
       D.A.D.O.S. 3rd Cav. Div.

I Units renders Indents as per attached C₃/3577.
   All Units are advised to have in possession
Parts I & II Priced Vocab. of Stores and A. Form G.1098

   II On receipt of Indent same is checked by
Chief Clerk to see that the nomenclature is correct;
that articles demanded are authorized in the
Mobolization Store tables of Unit and that Certificate at
top of form is correctly signed.

   III If all is in order Indent is given C 3 Indents
N° and signed by D.A.D.O.S. If not correct it is
returned to Unit with letter.

   IV Having been signed by D.A.D.O.S. the Original
Copy is forwarded to Base by D.A.D.O.S, all Bulk
Items having first being erased. The Duplicate Copy
is passed to the Warrant Officer of the Brigade to
which the Unit belongs and filed in the un-
-completed Indent Pad of that Unit. Bulk Items
are first marked D.B. which means entered in
Distribution list, and Certain important items such
as Binoculars are noted in Blue showing they have
been entered in Record of Certain important Issues.
This record is referred to by Chief Clerk when checking
Indents to see that no carelessness or waste of important
items is going on.

BULK ISSUES A. 3

Gly. Worc OB. 55. Due out Midday Thursday 15 July.
Gly . . . Arrive Monday 19-7-15.

Caps Service Dress. Summary of Indents for Bulk Issues.

CAPS S. D. SIZES.

UNITS	6	6 1/8	6 1/4	6 3/8	6 1/2	6 5/8	6 3/4	6 7/8	7	7 1/8	7 1/4	7 3/8	7 1/2	7 5/8	7 3/4		REMARKS
N.S.Y. 2715								2,1	2,1	9,1	11		5/7		5	12	
N.S.Y. 2481													+,+		1		
R.H.Q. 2720																	
N.S.Y. 3173															24		
R.M.Q. 3116								D	2,2,1	4,1	1,1				4		✱ Transferred to next Bulk
7 Sqn F10 3137								3,1	4,1	3					9		Sheet
8 Cav Fd A.C.S. 3105									3						3		
C B/M.Y 3107					1,1	2,2	2,10	5,1							20		
Am Col 3116							3,1	1,1							5		
C/M.Y 3202					3,4	8,1	5,2,1	1,1							23		
2./2.9 3203						1	10,1	1,1							15		
Hq 7 Cav B^th 3199							2,1								2		
Sub-total column					5,1	12,1	10,20	20,1	4,1						71		
Total Req^n A.2 55		-	-	-	6	22	17	51	6,5	18	-	-	4	-	1	-	Haste 5 or 6.
Receipt Voucher 2484		-	-	-	6	22	17	51	5,1	18	-	-	6	-	0	-	
Balance																	

TOTALS......

Y

WAR DIARY. Appendix I Sheet 3

on If he considers there is a doubt, unit is called upon
to account for the   demand.

  V The Staff Sergeant Clerk compiles the
Weekly Bulk lists. These are automatically closed
on afternoon of day when Bulk Demands are due
at Base. Sample of a Weekly Bulk Distribution
Statement attached "Y". This forms a permanent
record of issues made of Bulk Items in due course.

  VI After this, the total quantities is sent.
This list is ~~kept~~ kept by D.A.D.O.S. who takes it
to Station on the day stores are due. This
Programme of Issues from Base.

  VII On receipt of stores at Railhead they
are taken to the Divisional Distribution Point,
which is some shed or building as close to
Railhead as possible, providing roof from
Rain and safe lock up in case all stores received
cannot be loaded up on day of arrival.

  VIII Boxes and Bundles of each item are
opened and contents checked by number; if found
to agree, Bulk vouchers is signed and if necessary
to be returned to Base.

  IX Distribution then takes place. Labels for
each Class of Stores are made out quoting Indent
No., Unit name and nature of article and number
due out. The number required are called out, and
then the label is tied on to the Bundle, each in the
space reserved for that particular unit. The
distribution is carried on until stock received is
all gone. If more numbers of any item have been

Sheet 3. Appendix J

sent up than asked for. The overissue is shown on D.B. List, which then goes back to Office and instructions are given for distribution of Balance directly Units indent for them. In some cases issue can be made at once; in other cases it may be in store for a week or so before asked for; need for a lock-up store is therefore apparent.

X. After distribution has taken place, both D.B. stores and labelled detail stores are mustered by Warrant Officers in charge of Brigades who all meet at distribution point daily, and packages for each Unit are entered in their Army Book 108. Stores are then loaded up into lorries and distributed; receipts being obtained from Quarter Masters or Quarter Master Sergeants on the Original Copies of detailed vouchers. Indents are marked up at night for issues made during the day. Once a week Warrant Officers compare their uncompleted indents with Unit copies and settle any discrepancies before they get too old. The original copy of Voucher is endorsed I.M.U. which stands for "Indent marked up" and initialled by the Warrant Officer, and then returned to Office. Here they are registered and returned to Base. The duplicate copies are retained in Office and filed away with copy of Way Bill. If the train arrives in the morning, all stores are as a rule delivered to Units by that evening, and by next afternoon receipted detailed Vouchers endorsed I.M.U. are sent to Base.

Sheet 4 Appendix I.

XI Horseshoes on receipt are always stacked in the Goods Yard of the Station carefully arranged in sizes. The Divisional Railhead Representative keeps an eye on them, also the Railhead Police. Issues are made weekly to Units on those days most suitable to Transport and Brigade Warrant Officers. The day when no train arrives i.e. Sunday is favourite day for delivery of Horseshoes. A careful record of Issues is kept.

XII Double issues of Detail Stores from Base sometimes occur. If these are of a nature that is constantly being demanded such as Farrier Tools, Draught Poles, Saddlery parts, they are kept as extra Item stock, and these Items are used to meet incoming Indents, there being considerable saving in time over issues to be made. They will have to be required at early date. They are returned to Base at once as it is most important that no stores not actually required for Units are kept at Railheads.

T.W.S.

Army Form C. 2118.

WAR DIARY
or
INTELLIGENCE SUMMARY.
(Erase heading not required.)

August 1915

Major. A.F.N. BARRON. R.A.
Ind: bri: Sept.

D.A.D.O.S. 3rd Cavalry Division

From 1.8.15   To. 31.8.15

Place	Date	Hour	Summary of Events and Information	Remarks and references to Appendices

WAR DIARY
or
INTELLIGENCE SUMMARY

Army Form C. 2118

Place	Date	Hour	Summary of Events and Information	Remarks and references to Appendices
HEURINGHEM	Aug '15 1.		From DADOS 1st Indian Cav. Divn. Took over duties of DADOS 3rd Cav Divn from Major T.B.A. LEAHY. AOD. The 3rd Cav Divn is at railhead is at STEINBEKE my stores is at HAZEBROUCK	
	2.		Taken for change of railhead to ARQUES came today. I went in to settle for billets for the detachment and arrange a store for my stores	
			HAZEBROUCK	
	4.		Moved my stores from STEINBEKE to ARQUES. This took my 6 lorries two trips on Lhasa a very large reserve of Smoke helmets out respirators (1 per man sack)	
FAUQUEMBERG	5.		Division moved from present billets to an area south of THÉROUANNE – AIRE road and East of River AA	
	11, 12, 14		Inspected the explosive fronts of the division. Found the storage arrangements generally satisfactory. But a quantity required refacing	

Signed: [signature]
DADOS 3rd Cav Divn

Army Form C. 2118.

WAR DIARY
or
INTELLIGENCE SUMMARY.
(Erase heading not required.)

September 1915

Major A.F.N. BARRON. R.A.
2nd Ord Dept.

D.A.D.O.S. 3rd Cavalry Division

From 1.9.15   To 30.9.15

Instructions regarding War Diaries and Intelligence Summaries are contained in F.S. Regs., Part II. and the Staff Manual respectively. Title pages will be prepared in manuscript.

Place	Date	Hour	Summary of Events and Information	Remarks and references to Appendices

Army Form C. 2118

WAR DIARY
or
INTELLIGENCE SUMMARY.
(Erase heading not required.)

Instructions regarding War Diaries and Intelligence Summaries are contained in F. S. Regs., Part II. and the Staff Manual respectively. Title pages will be prepared in manuscript.

Place	Date	Hour	Summary of Events and Information	Remarks and references to Appendices
FAUQUEMBERGUE	Sept 1/15	8 to 9	Inspected the explosives of the division - the O.C. Austin Park had his puncture stored in a temporary magazine with bombs, grenades, detonators and ammunition. I gave orders that this must not be done. I saw every lot of the explosives in charge of regiment, and gave orders by phone that was unserviceable and to make up all deficiencies - the 10th Hussars had had a case of matches reserved loose and in ordinary trade wooden boxes. I gave orders that the proper tin boxes must be indented for at once. Lieut. S. E. ALLEN AOD (temporary) turned. He is to be instructed in the duties of a A.D.O.D. and when fit to carry them out a report to be made to A.O's Cav Corps.	
WESTREHEM	21.		"B" echelon transport of the division moved to WESTREHEM (DELETTES) The 6th & 8th Cav. Bdes. to the BOIS des DAMES. HQrs to LABOUSSIERE. The 7th Bde left to join 2nd Army.	[signature] Lt Col 3 Cav Div

Army Form C. 2118

WAR DIARY
or
INTELLIGENCE SUMMARY.
(Erase heading not required.)

Instructions regarding War Diaries and Intelligence Summaries are contained in F. S. Regs., Part II. and the Staff Manual respectively. Title pages will be prepared in manuscript.

Place	Date	Hour	Summary of Events and Information	Remarks and references to Appendices
	Sept 1/15			
WESTREHEM.	22.		Staff Sergt. SMYTHE M.A.O.E (new force) joined to take over duties of chief clerk from Condr. STAPLE ordered to BOULOGNE.	
LABOUSSIERE	24		Moved to the Qrs of the division as I found that I could not keep properly in touch with them from "B" Eschelon. No to bring with Hd Qrs I was not informed of change of railhead. Condr STAPLE came up with me. Lieut ALLEN with remainder of detachment went to AIRE which is present railhead.	
	26		Sub Condr. HICKS. detailed with 2 lorries to 2nd Army to do Duty with 9th Cav Bde. Remainder of Division moved forward to MARZINGARBE. I remained behind with Hd Qr of Divn.	
	27.		No stores from Calais for last 4 days owing to misunderstanding of COO as to which railhead they should be sent although I had personally told him to send all to AIRE (Cav Corps railhead). I sent out Condr Sturgeon with a lorry to Calais to bring up a supply of oil grease bull tongs etc. which we badly wanted also for 2 machine guns tripods & lost by RHGs at LOOS.	

AMurray
BSM 3rd Cav Bde

1577 Wt. W10791/1773 500,000 1/15 D. D. & L. A.D.S.S./Forms/C. 2118.

Army Form C. 2118

WAR DIARY
or
INTELLIGENCE SUMMARY.
(Erase heading not required.)

Instructions regarding War Diaries and Intelligence Summaries are contained in F. S. Regs., Part II. and the Staff Manual respectively. Title pages will be prepared in manuscript.

Place	Date	Hour	Summary of Events and Information	Remarks and references to Appendices
LABOUSSIERE	Sept /15 28		Supply of stores have begun to arrive again. Since the division has been in action, the ordnance lorries have gone out with the supply column. If they did not do so they would probably go by wrong roads and black traffic. They might lose touch with the horse transport efforts and in case of break down would be helpless	
	29th		The division was relieved from LOOS last night and returned to bivouacs in the BOIS des DAMES. I have visited advanced H.Q. each day division has been in action by doing this I have been able to arrange for stores required in the field and thus save several hours by not waiting for actual demands from in-deck. The necessity of keeping advance lorries with supply column was proved last night. The troops moved in the middle of the night and it was only the fact that they were with the supply column that the advance lorries arrived at rendezvous this morning. Also the 8th Bde lorry broke a spring and was brought along by the break down lorry of the column	

[signature]
D.A.D.S.
3rd Cavy [?]

S E ALLEN Lieut
A.O.D.

Army Form C. 2118.

WAR DIARY
or
INTELLIGENCE SUMMARY
(Erase heading not required.)

November 5th to 30th 1915

Instructions regarding War Diaries and Intelligence Summaries are contained in F. S. Regs., Part II. and the Staff Manual respectively. Title pages will be prepared in manuscript.

Hour, Date, Place	Summary of Events and Information	Remarks and references to Appendices
November 5th Ypres	On 27 [?] Bombs [?] and our [?] [?]	
6th	Nothing to report	
7th	Fort Rathcool fired a short [?]	
8th	Nothing to report	
9th	Fort Rathcool our [?] fired together [?]	
10th	No [?] to [?] in [?] all day	
11th	Nothing to report	
12th	Major [?] relieved [?] R.H. So. [?] Major P. appears in 6th Brigade	
13th	Inspected dump & explosives. 7th Brigade — previous [?]	
14th	Ammunition Military & Petroleum 8th Brigade	
15th	Reported A. og. [?] in [?] [?] of [?] — animals [?] [?] to [?]	
16th	First Battalion Boat Circle [?] appearance commander at [?]	
17th	[?] [?] Close [?] as [?] wants. [?] Late	
17th	Nothing to report. Boat Railhead out [?] [?] in [?] & [?]	
19th	Boat [?] of [?] Force that will be [?] in line (1 not western.	
19th	Fort Rathcool [?] fire from 10 [?] to motors & targets [?] 8.9713.	
20th	Normal [?] A short	
21st	Although it not railhead boats as not [?] worth [?] [?] [?] [?]	
21st	Saw G. Sgm. 3rd Dragoon [?]. Enquire that the drills there [?] to	
22nd	[?] before our line intended	
23rd	But Railhead as explosion. Out of [?] into demanded [?] of	
1st	Saw A & G.S.S. no time to [?] as it officer all day, out & [?]	
25th	A.A.G.Sh.S [?] our [?] [?] [?] to [?] on a [?] & [?]	
26th	But railhead both circle [?] of [?] [?] our [?] of [?]	
1st	Saw G.m. Lieut. [?] [?] — bomber out [?] no [?] of [?] met	
27th	to hold 25 units , out [?]	
28th	Normal — nothing to report	
29th	Fort Railhead [?] [?] fire into non Drag. Dept.	
30th	to [?] [?] been. Saw G.G.S.R.C. [?] to [?]	

R. Allen Lt
D.A.D. b. S
32nd Cav. Div.

S E ALLEN Lieut
R.O.D

D.A.D.O.S. 3 Cav. Dn
Nov + Dec /15
Vol II - A

Army Form C. 2118.

WAR DIARY
or
INTELLIGENCE SUMMARY

(Erase heading not required.)

DECEMBER 1st to 31st

Hour, Date, Place	Summary of Events and Information	Remarks and references to Appendices
December 1st Troyes	Lieut Rathbone on leave upon the C.O. "S.M.I." normal.	
1a	Troops arrive in camp & on G.M.S.	
2a	Inspection of Bain Row & ambulance 300 a culturity	
4th	Lieut Rathbone on a horse of bread home transport & ARO ones etc.	
5th	Saw CO. G.M.I. and discussed possibility of reducing units & am comm & park & bathers and called at time of with & an inspected there.	
6th	Nothing to report	
7th	Lieut Rathbone inspecting Rose of Ges. Mob. Portable	
8th	No turn on & afric all day	
9th	Some visits to them au mot seen gallay min as not then	
10th	Witness theore of explosives 4th Brigade wagons Billitos	
11th	Inspection Raices of Septentive 7th Brigade wet without inspection Battery for horses of 8th Brigade big wet without	
12th	Repairs inspection of C.C. & G.M.S. Lieut Col. Bishop S.C. C.O.S.	
13th	Lieut Rathbone leaves morning up and roots bathose wood do not	
14th	Am General Pitchery to report horse lorse loot in two	
15th	Saw C.C.G.M.S. & Commander upon of Horses at Ferme Bihuss	
16th	Lieut Rathbone home there up pathers & App 8 & 9 & 10	
17th	Normal nothing to report	
18th	Normal nothing to report	
19th	General without to report	
20th	Lieut without on a called a unit of 4th Brigade & cavert	
21st	then forge of rel F. a.b. G. = Cam. S. cottons absorbing t not expense	
22nd		
23rd		
24th	Just a tour with a report homens as a return normal	
25th		
31st		

S. Allen Lt
D.A.D.O.S.
3d Corps Dn

Tend 2 Bathore outfits to units of 8th Brigade Sa. A. B. & G. M.G. normal
S. Allen Lt
D.A.D.O.S.
3d Corps Dn

WAR DIARY

OF

D.A.D.O.S

3RD CAVALRY DIVISION

JAN - DEC 1915

(Oct. missing)

S E ALLEN Lieut
~~D.A.D~~ A.O.D

Instructions regarding War Diaries and Intelligence Summaries are contained in F. S. Regs., Part II. and the Staff Manual respectively. Title pages will be prepared in manuscript.

WAR DIARY
or
INTELLIGENCE SUMMARY

(Erase heading not required.)

Army Form C. 2118.

JANUARY 1918

Hour, Date, Place	Summary of Events and Information	Remarks and references to Appendices
January 1st Ytres	Railhead moved to Beaulin [illegible] temporarily	
2nd "	Dismounted Brigade ready to join Dismounted Division	
3rd "	7th Dismounted Brigade join Dismounted Division	
4th "	Railhead moved to Montauban difficult to obtain stores for urgent stores.	
5th "	Saw A.A. & Q.M.G. at Railhead received 900 bags more which I 200 released locally on authority	
6th "	In visits ordered many units accept second shirt in lieu	
7th "	Normal nothing to report	
8th "	Just ready to Dismounted Div with stores which had come to	
9th "	Division completed with P.H. helmet and supplies at Railhead. mentioned in store	
10th "	Normal demands for stores not falling off enough	
11th "	Saw Q.M. Master of 6 Brigade with a view to reducing demands.	
12th "	Inspected storage of explosives 6th Brigade at Railhead	
13th "	Inspected storage of explosives 7th Brigade "	
14th "	Inspected storage of explosives 8th Brigade	
15th "	Reported inspection to A.A. & Q.M.G.	
16th "	Normal nothing to report	
18th "	Orderly [illegible] up at Railhead no visits no other leave due out.	
19th "	Saw A.A. & Q.M.G. furnished list of special stores in possession of units	
20th "	Sent up more blankets to Dismounted Division on A.A. & Q.M.G. instructions	
21st "	Normal nothing to report	
22nd "	Applied for additional lorry as in the event of a move carriage of Gum boots, Smoke helmets and other than Standard would be difficult.	
23rd "	Nothing to report	
24th "	Extra lorry not allowed. Warning given exposed helmets.	
25th "	Visit Railhead and aim to meet lorries stores required.	
26th "	Dismounted Brigade still away slight falling off in demands.	
27th "	Normal nothing to report	
28th "	A.D.O.S. met me at Railhead inspected dumps and expressed satisfaction	
29th "	Saw A.A. & Q.M.G. at Railhead General stores up & made dumps out of [illegible]	
30th "	Normal nothing to report	
31st "	Saw A.A. & Q.M.G. at Railhead, normal	R Allen Lt D.A.D.O.S 3rd Cav Div

1247 W 3299 200,000 (E) 8/14 J.B.C. & A. Forms/C. 2118/11.

SE ALLEN LT
A.O.D

Army Form C. 2118.

WAR DIARY
or
INTELLIGENCE SUMMARY

(Erase heading not required.)

4 January 1st – 29 th

Hour, Date, Place	Summary of Events and Information	Remarks and references to Appendices
7 January 1st 4 aug t~	Normal working & report	
2nd	Demands getting 60 over Railhead and bought supplies for fellow known.	
3rd	Went Railhead normal	
4th	Saw C.O. & S.M.S. and Railhead. home from two package of Troops Papers	
5th	working & report	
6th	Demands considerably reduced. Otherwise normal.	
7th	Saw C.O. & S.M.S. Inspected Vet units. Rcv'd mix for certain Rcm 6	
8th	Normal working & report	Equipment would Otis Room
9th	No truck up to Office all day.	
10th	Saw C.O. & S.M.S. went to southern arm inspected stores of supplies to Bri...	
11th	Inspected stores of Supplies of 4th Brigade. also went Railhead	
12th	Inspected Recep. of Supplies of 8th Brigade. Unit Confirm of Stin	
13th	Inspected Recep. of Supplies of 8th Brigade. Str. on Maps. Ry cont.	
14th	Inspected Transportation & C.O. & P.M.G. Complaints received re boots & U.S.	
15th	Working & Report	military Rep cases replies reported C.D.O.S
16th	Saw C.O. & S.M.R. furnished list of Brads Plain Mill ripened & complete	
17th	Went Railhead item arrived for Dismounted Brigade Sent Mechanical	
18th	The truck up.	Been acceptable item by lorry
19th	Written up Saw C.O. & S.M.S. Demand for item advice.	
20th	Dismounted Brigade retn.	
21st	All Good Plain left by Dismounted Brigade.	
22nd	No issues & note bottles rate come up from Basa	
23rd	Saw C.O. & P.M.S. one Railhead. Cancelled all intelligence	
	returns for into intense until statement	
24th	Went Railhead demands for Otis & return to 7th Army	
25th	Normal demands for Vetinary. Rather “light”.	
26th	Asiatica 1284 Pairs Boots Th42 from units out of ft. 1500 issued	
27th	Working & Report Arrangement of Boot one clothing removed from Ch. Depot	
28th	Saw C.O. & P.M.S. Rain lost of thread Mun. left Behind & lot	
29th	Saw C.D.O.S. O/c brought Plans tire Pats for carrying machine	
	Gun, Different types + attachments for test & report	

N Allen H
To A to S.
3rd Can Div

Forms/C. 2118/11.

S E ALLEN Capt
G.O.D

Army Form C. 2118.

WAR DIARY
or
INTELLIGENCE SUMMARY

(Erase heading not required.)

MARCH 1914 31st

Instructions regarding War Diaries and Intelligence Summaries are contained in F. S. Regs., Part II. and the Staff Manual respectively. Title pages will be prepared in manuscript.

Hour, Date, Place	Summary of Events and Information	Remarks and references to Appendices
March 1st Fuupo	Saw A.A. & Q.M.G. re approval of forming the Ammunition Park into Railhead Sect. A.D.O.S. Ammunition Park	
2.00		
3.00	Saw A.A. & Q.M.G. Inspected Transport of Brigade Sec. of Field Ambulance	
4.00	D.D.O.S. to inspect Transport told us there to be in a position to take A.O.C. P.O.S. approval	
5.00	Arrival of Acting Adjutant. A lot of Text? inspected Ammunition Park submitted to A.D.O.S. & Q.M.G. cont. Brush for clothing on 4 Stutton Fund with Camp equipment approved.	
6.00	Saw Q.M.C. & Q.M.G.S. inst. Railhead cont.	
7.00	Tent Brown at Markham there 4 days. Because firm is dying out	
8.00	Army contingent received Clothing for own Clothing issued from C.O.C. Capt. Item passed at the same as the Give if qualified to use work	
9.00	Saw G.C.C. & Q.M.? int Railhead	
10.00	Hospital Foot Train 6 9L Brigade loss ?? Brigade and ?? out Railhead supp.	
11.00		
12.00	Tent Birthcare Inspection of companies of Brigade. All A clothing disposed	
13.00	Saw C.D.O.S. inspected blocks of ammunition of Brigade out Railhead	
14.00	Arrival of meeting of Hosp.	
15.00	Saw A.A. & Q.M.G. approved of am inspection	
16.00	Birmingham firm to have to see Capt down and sense meeting ?	
17.00	Se A.A. & Q.M.G. receives letter of winter Clothing went out ? ?? 4. Staff	
18.00	Called for Ammunition Park for Ammunition Park received out Railhead	
19.00	20 hrs Report	
20.00	No truck up on officer down morning Cas Copr ?? Hosp firm train firm	
21.00	Test Railhead called to unit ? of ? Transport ?? ? ? of ? Brigade	
22.00	arrival out G.B.O.C. mountable Rahbe	
23.00	arrived out Railhead	
24.00	See A.A. & Q.M.S. all units informed of Medical form	
25.00	?? from Italian & informed ink Transport ?? ? on Equipment of 1 2 A not	
26.00	Due D.A. & Q.M.S. Horses inspection 850 mountable Sense uniform	
27.00	Q.M.G. 2 inspect out Railhead. Saw 3 A D. & 4 H.M. ?c ?? F.S. S	
28.00	Saw G.D.O.S. Can't return 6 trucks ?? for watering again.	
29.00	Convoy out Railhead.	
30.00	Cas out 5 cars in Ordnance	
31.00	Ca. out 6 cars in Ordnance. ?? See ?. Brigade loss 2 brygone type one ammun & 6	
	Convoy Ordnance Brigade Sec out Railhead. Saw A.D.O.S. Down also	

S Allen Capt
D.A.D.O.S.
31st Cav Div.

S E A L L E N Capt
A.O.D

Army Form C. 2118.

WAR DIARY
or
INTELLIGENCE SUMMARY
(Erase heading not required.)

April 1st — 30th

Instructions regarding War Diaries and Intelligence Summaries are contained in F. S. Regs., Part II. and the Staff Manual respectively. Title pages will be prepared in manuscript.

Hour, Date, Place	Summary of Events and Information	Remarks and references to Appendices
April 1st 7.15 p.m.	20 Imp lorries PLS of Equipment for Camp in Hotel Return from Regina from T.B.m.	
2nd	Saw G.O.C. q.m.g. Ordnance distribution.	
3rd	Divisional school of Instruction formed at Tramcourt went 2 additional	
4th	Unit Calais Engineer Camps Troop assist for Ramilly Camp also 200	
5th	Normal nothing of report. Equipment for facing Malt Rimeux from Etm.	
6th	Went Railhead normal	
7th	See G.O.C. q.m.g. the figures that of all items since I taking of production	
8th	Nothing to report	
9th	Saw G.O.C. q.m.g. Supplied list of items required for camp unit	
10th	Went Southern inspected storage of Canadian 6th Brigade. Canadian Brigade	
11th	See G.A. q.m.g. Supplied 2 months list of B.M. stores + front arg Brigade list	
12th	Nim arm.	
13th	Inspect Shops of Explosion 4th Brig for B.M. & bn & Canadian Spirit Compat.	
14th	Nothing to report	
15th	Report Inspection of D.A.D.O.S went Railhead Met all Jam bops	
16th	Units Except Supply Col the Rest were their Firm B.D.S Front Concept	
17th	Normal Nothing to report	for Musial with	
18th	Saw D.D.O.S for Drakart Saw A.A. q.m.g. S. in Office all day.	
19th	See A.D.O.S Rfurm Boots Clothing other Units also I Bn.	
20th	Went Railhead all Units receiving every Difference By Units.	
21st	Nothing to report	
22nd	Follow Mq of Hospitis Div. Capt Seadler Received Returned distribution from
23rd	Normal Nothing Railhead nothing to report	G.A.G.q.m.g.
24th	Saw A.A. q.m.g. Over bad Partridebilly Pat Salon factory I went office after
25th	Went Railhead all camp Equipment up from T.B.m	Tea Kitz Issued 2 high + 4.5 Disputable for
26th	See G. Bn. on East in Spew nothing to report	work
27th	Went Railhead new camped From armament to Bronnville framed
28th		our arrived at Corbie
29th	On train nothing during the time of report camp at A.e.f
30th		morning new camps + railhead at him Schnapplunh. Visit. Reported distribution to Hol. Hiker Sie South (Seadler). Comon

S Allen Capt
D.D.O.S
1st Cav Div

Army Form C. 2118.

Instructions regarding War Diaries and Intelligence Summaries are contained in F. S. Regs., Part II. and the Staff Manual respectively. Title pages will be prepared in manuscript.

WAR DIARY
or
INTELLIGENCE SUMMARY.
(Erase heading not required.)

BANDS
3 Cav DM

May 1st – 16th

May 1916

Vol XI

Place	Date	Hour	Summary of Events and Information	Remarks and references to Appendices
Fryps	1st		Went Taithaee afterwards saw units of 3 Brigade	
"	2nd		In office all day	
"	3rd		Usual routine	
"	4th		Saw A.A. & Q.M.S. went Taithaee normal	
"	5th		Went to Camp at Tatha	
"	6th		Gathering & report	
"	7th		Usual. Then up saw A.A. & Q.M.S. Cav. writers incidents at Taithaee	
"	8th		19th Div. Cyclist to Lyons Divsn. as a Cav. Tour.	
"	9th		Went Taithaee saw all units 6th Brigade and fourth Brigade returns normal	
"	10th		Normal work routine	
"	11th		Dinner & men sent for training area in G.S.	
"	12th		Saw A.A. & Q.M.S. saw Taithaee normal	
"	13th		Saw all units of 7th Brigade	
"	14th		Seen at orders	
"	15th		Divisn. orders & O.C. Tyres for Training	
"	16th		Gathering & report no rides & seleeras to order the whom	

Army Form C. 2118.

WAR DIARY
or
INTELLIGENCE SUMMARY.
(Erase heading not required.)

May 17 - 31. 17

Instructions regarding War Diaries and Intelligence Summaries are contained in F. S. Regs., Part II. and the Staff Manual respectively. Title pages will be prepared in manuscript.

Place	Date	Hour	Summary of Events and Information	Remarks and references to Appendices
Faya	17		At the arrival at Faithar & a advance of Building area	
"	18		} Nothing to Report.	
"	19		}	
"	20		}	
"	21		Visit Union & sa area after training	
"	22		Saw A.D.O.S. Limber Wagon has not sufficiently strong and for the	
"	23		" " " " they carry	
"	24		See A.O. & G.P.S. out Rations normal	
"	25		In Office nothing to Report.	
"	26		State of N. C Then turn convoys & supplies from Base Stores Faithar	
"	27		own at " " "	
"	28		Went off to camp at a Faithar also both M.T. & O.T. Turns to	
"	29		Rations & report.	
"	30		Called a A.D.O.S. supplies and demands normal	
"	31		Saw A.O. & G.P.S. out rations also reserve rations	

C. Ab Capt a.o.D
D.A.D.O.S
3rd Cav Div

Army Form C. 2118.

WAR DIARY
of
INTELLIGENCE SUMMARY.
(Erase heading not required.)

PART II. Jan 1st to 16th
3 Cav Div Vol 12

June 1916.

Instructions regarding War Diaries and Intelligence Summaries are contained in F. S. Regs., Part II. and the Staff Manual respectively. Title pages will be prepared in manuscript.

Place	Date	Hour	Summary of Events and Information	Remarks and references to Appendices
Fayt	1st		Went to Camps at a Faithem one at their up	
"	2nd		Saw A.A + Q.M.S nothing to report	
"	3rd		Called on A.D.O.S and Faithem Reserve Trenchs and Chateau Belonte etc	
"	4th		Nothing to report	
"	5th		Bought one jumper for machine and Faithea	
"	6th		Called in all units of 8th Brigade	
"	7th		No car in office all day	
"	8th		No car in office all day	
"	9th		Went Faithear saw units of 7th Bde also A.C + Q.M.S.	
"	10th		Ambarri Rese cycling with our cycle neck difficult to obtain	
"	11th		Saw units of 7th Brigade	
"	12th		Nothing to report	
"	13th		Canvassed nothing to report	
"	14th		Went Paris up where A.A + Q.M.S + Saw D.D.O instructing units & was Paris	
"	15th		The Austrian armies in communication to Lebania. Would raid of Paris	
"	16th		Court all nothing to report	

Army Form C. 2118.

WAR DIARY
OR
INTELLIGENCE SUMMARY.
(Erase heading not required.)

Instructions regarding War Diaries and Intelligence Summaries are contained in F. S. Regs., Part II. and the Staff Manual respectively. Title pages will be prepared in manuscript.

June 17th to 31st

Place	Date	Hour	Summary of Events and Information	Remarks and references to Appendices
Fuyn	17th		Normal	
"	18th		Posting & Returns	
"	19th		Saw A.D.O.S. about Railhead	
"	20th		At A.D.M.S. and arrange to clear line from B.T.S.S. & 22T.D.	
"	21st		Saw A.D. & G.D.S. in office all day	
"	22nd		Divisional Boot Repair Shop	
"	23rd		Normal	
"	24th		Payments Company Armourers dumps. Packhorses & men	
"	25th		Division move to DOMART. Lorries not sufficient to carry kits 6.30 cwt.	
DOMART	26th		Rain again at Divisional Railhead to Regimental stores from 3 our finish solved	
C. Newville	27th		Railhead Frevent	
"	28th		Saw the coals from distribution. Took again Boots for disinfection for Mitchinson	
"	29th		Lorries not up to Col. B. reserve rations etc.	
"	30th		Drove an went all day all complete but two Boots oil silvent at A.O.D Zahalpa Coln	
"	31st		Arrange to continue to make another dismounting in A.O.D Zahalpa Coln	

P. Allen Capt. A.O.D
D.A.D.O.S
31st Cav Di.

Army Form C. 2118.

D.A.D.O.S. 3 Cav Div

WAR DIARY
or
INTELLIGENCE SUMMARY.
(Erase heading not required.)

July 1st — 31st
July 1916

Vol/3

Place	Date	Hour	Summary of Events and Information	Remarks and references to Appendices
La Neuville	1st		Pleasing C. to Harris Fisham. Complete the arrangements of the 8th Public Forces returns on the issue of Gas masks from the reserve arranged for Reserve Sac Garrison to meet the Reserve Regulation at 2 hours notice will consist all 5 a.m. many Divisions massing on a battle field the plain.	
"	2nd		Visited D.D.O.S, Reserve Army. Returned to Capt. Smith. Brittain AA+QMS. Rawn to 12th Cav. O.C. to be appointed will take effect to Reserve Reserve Reinforcements. I saw 7002 Dep. Man. 9th Composite received.	
"	3rd			
Hallencourt	4th		From A. Hallencourt across the Churche at Molie.	
"	5th		S.L. 30 Cart. Korken West Refilment 2 men Were unable cannot get the stores the Army was a man can them with Cp. Zelmel Reserve Fester the full cover being seen. Within Loryal through a machine order. This I mean to rather Stores present in a troop this is there in action.	
"	6th			
"	7th		Finding Subsequently also Capt. Moore this Farriers were consider there were the subsidies are on went the man movements	
"	8th			
"	9th		From 4 Dague	
Daours	10th		Dump one tradition of H.Q. Rams Jorn the withdraw 50.	
"	11th		The cost to Zundern ark not up to scale to Serrace to a field amer.	
"	12th		Spare parts for Hotchkiss Guns different letter. From the Division. 1 per from stores to 2 per. Line Baltheon Battery to report.	

Army Form C. 2118.

WAR DIARY
or
INTELLIGENCE SUMMARY.
(Erase heading not required.)

Instructions regarding War Diaries and Intelligence Summaries are contained in F.S. Regs., Part II. and the Staff Manual respectively. Title pages will be prepared in manuscript.

July 13th to 25th

Place	Date	Hour	Summary of Events and Information	Remarks and references to Appendices
Dacca	13th		Usual visits by men. Hotchkiss Team all in also after whole elements. Received one Hotchkiss Gun.	
"	14th		On 45f from rattier after 4.30 a.m. in office all day. Chat to day church parade.	
"	15th		Bn Rovnelli. Received 276 also bulls. Heavy rain about nothing to report.	
"	16th		Hotchkiss Team 27 recruits and visits. Bombing drill up to 9 pm reyment.	
"	17th		Usual Sho near Bn Perparates as NSF sent them. Compl: all that they cannot carry them.	
"	18th		Hotchkiss Team 27 recruits one Lieuwer & Co'S Batallery then complete the Divs in 12 Am reyment and Pl B Battlery for same.	
"	19th		Chipra 9 Intrs 160 recruits. Brown Drive to Hill Khan Pal Parueburg NSF refitippers. Nothing to report until the up also from on arrival Lances 1108.	
"	20th			
"	21st		Lieut Hawkings 300 men met and took am up and stay Gun from Jailhuice. Then came out of room and started running of horses the topic to dear effect no team for	
"	22nd		Usual Men. Also Bombthrow to reads and Capt Mackin honoured.	
"	23rd		Phol Patrol. 1500 received and aristobretion. Signals cte out except both via (a) it went to tent DRLS. Colonel for this & Co conference in wiring.	
"	24th		Lieut Dargner & Pl 80 Mardli & letters from Mrs Crum affairs of Blankingly batta.	
"	25th		Usual Phol. up also from Hill Khan Gun from Park. Got Dm Clothing no Syx - pacified they make no distribution sufficient	

Army Form C. 2118.

WAR DIARY
or
INTELLIGENCE SUMMARY.

(Erase heading not required.)

Continued
July 25th & 31st

Instructions regarding War Diaries and Intelligence Summaries are contained in F. S. Regs., Part II. and the Staff Manual respectively. Title pages will be prepared in manuscript.

Place	Date	Hour	Summary of Events and Information	Remarks and references to Appendices
DACORS	26th		From at Authim 4 eprit.	
	27th		Order sand 115 Vhr complete repairable. All limbers ready for moving, which is rather Matrials Sections.	
	28th		Took 200 reins also material for flooring distribution received from AA & PAF.	
	29th		Limt trailleus in Epsom all day with 4 eprit.	
	30th		Came to wait Dumon Division.	
	31st		Limt Valtause and angot & thirty brenks no. & mos tradhaeu with wet mt to the place in was & mon eneups Amepin & two entter bent & one spae with Shti & mes valhaeu for 20 CLT touris also sufficient	

J. Allen
DADOS
3rd Cav. Div.

Army Form C. 2118.

Instructions regarding War Diaries and Intelligence Summaries are contained in F. S. Regs., Part II. and the Staff Manual respectively. Title pages will be prepared in manuscript.

WAR DIARY
or
INTELLIGENCE SUMMARY.
(Erase heading not required.)

F.S. Aim Capt
D.A.D.O.S. A.O.D.
3rd Cav. Div.

August 1st – 16th

Place	Date	Hour	Summary of Events and Information	Remarks and references to Appendices
L Quesnoy	1		Division moves from DAOURS to LE QUESNOY.	
VRENCH	2		Move from Le Quesnoy to VRENCH	
"	3		Sent lorry back to pick up balance of that morning on guard	
Longueau	4		Move from VRENCH to Longueau	
Frise	5		From Longueau to Frise	
"	6		Sent lorries back to bring over balance of Amn	
"	7		Went back to Longueau town. Amn. forward balance of that	
"	8		To Longueau Depot. Orderlies and spoke to Corps Inspector	
"	9		Thursday met Corps K. coin. also on arrest from Base	
"	10		Journey all day. Can't walk one in all. A talk on aman	
"	11		Office at Tramcourt. In C.C. + 9M 2nd CDOS. Capt Laveley	
"	12		R.O.C. interest Boscal Impress Holden Sea Padraddy also 6.7.03	
"	13		To Calais with bales of Hadden left one top.	
"	14		Sunval	
"	15		To dub, received hat for C.D.O.S. and A.D. + 9M R.	
"	16		To Office all day. No car.	

WAR DIARY
INTELLIGENCE SUMMARY

Army Form C. 2118.

August 1915

Place	Date	Hour	Summary of Events and Information	Remarks and references to Appendices
HQ	17		Visit of Divisor Director & upkeep references	
"	18		Journal	
"	19		R.L. Nathan came up & met A.D.O.S.	
"	20		Office & report	
"	21st		Call at G. Office. Went on bus to Hort Amazon P.S.	
"	22		Out all day. Officer of... Gas dumps & place to camp P.S.	
"	23		& Calm & that for enforce overflow & Hellehin Type	
"	24		Saw I thought & 4th G.H.Q. Gen. Inspection & G.D.O.S.	
"	25		Visit Zone Horse Pro Reynolds chief put too Helleshin Type at grahi	
"	26/25		R. Box wire Zone Emperor Call Hellehin Type armore & uphau wowd move	
"	27		met Nathan & report	
"	28		In Office all day. indent Gallup M.J.	
"	29		Sir. A.C. +9 to S.O. went took call A.D.O.S.	
"	30		On Saltrico armoriar P.S.P. armoury	
"	31		Normal	

R. Allan Capt.
A.O.D
DADOS
3rd Cav. Div.

Army Form C. 2118.

WAR DIARY
or
INTELLIGENCE SUMMARY.

September 1st – 24th

S. E. Allen Capt
A.O.D
D A D O S
3rd Class Div

Vol 1

(Erase heading not required.)

Place	Date	Hour	Summary of Events and Information	Remarks and references to Appendices
Fauq–	1–9–10		During this date I saw no threat filth. The Division completed and sent out a stationery return was low. I saw G.O.Q.M.G daily and go to 2 withdraw this weeks 460 D.O.S squads, Division on Maison Confieur I come back there	
Mais Confieur	11th			
Billy les Farm	12		Visited Maison Confieur & Billy les Farmer	
	14th		Redrew visits and find for London Reff before & back	
Daour	15th		Saw from Billy les Farmer & Daour	
	16th		find back at Louvre & Carry general the	
	17th		Do not consider it safe to recoup for the horses & from this & be lost	
	18th		as truck couren lin may complete	
	19th		Truck and all tires fast out 4 units.	
	20th		from a c willing & spot.	
	21st		Through truck comvir pop back and trace up between 8 times	
	22nd		from from Daour & Le Quesnoy	
	23rd		from Le Quesnoy & Toker Z- Brand	
	24th		from John – & Daour & Brouillie.	

Army Form C. 2118.

WAR DIARY
or
INTELLIGENCE SUMMARY.

(Erase heading not required.)

Instructions regarding War Diaries and Intelligence [September]
Summaries are contained in F. S. Regs., Part II.
and the Staff Manual respectively. Title pages 24 & 30
will be prepared in manuscript.

Place	Date	Hour	Summary of Events and Information	Remarks and references to Appendices
	25		Sent out to all horses & every forward horse	
	26		No truth in the call at G Officer in C.C. & Q.m.S.	
	27		The call at Hooper at Horse Coup at Horse in	
	28		Particularly amount of Pan & these to meet all	
	30		26th no disease in cattle. Horses without support	

D. Ellis Capt
a. o. P
D H D o E
3rd Cavalry Div

42/8

D.A.G.
3rd Echelon

Attached are my original copies of War Diary for October November and December 1916

S Allen Capt
D A D O S
3rd Cav Div
& Sept.

19/1/17

August Still due

WAR DIARY or INTELLIGENCE SUMMARY

Army Form C. 2118.

S.E. Allen Capt C.O.D
A.D.S.S
3rd Cav Div

October 1st – 31st

Place	Date	Hour	Summary of Events and Information	Remarks and references to Appendices
BREVILLERS	1st		Railhead Hucclecote. Men Office visit QDVS & APM.	
	2nd		To DQ Office afterward to Railhead and return to Cos regiments	
	3, 4, 5		For men other than clerks unable to go out owing to "Alerma".	
	6th		To A Railhead and various old indents and 24 hr Rtn	
	7th		Nothing to report.	
	8th		Saw Staff Captain 6th Brigade re Embarkation of Horse regiments	
	9th		No car in Office all day but met DQ Office & mess ADoS.	
	10th		Normal routine to report.	
	11th		Visited railhead and part of DQ Office out of day in Office	
	12th		At Railhead letter visited units of 7th Brigade	
	13th		Went to 155th pm to furnish present Stow returned to DQ Office	
	14th		To Office all morning visited railhead and received part of Plan	
	15th		Nothing to report.	
	16th		Go back up visitors to Office.	
	17th		Co the A.A & Q.M.S. that C.O. of regiments furnish first all indents	
	18th		Demand for their Cos heavy return then signed & quarter master	

Army Form C. 2118.

WAR DIARY
or
INTELLIGENCE SUMMARY.
(Erase heading not required.)

Instructions regarding War Diaries and Intelligence Summaries are contained in F. S. Regs., Part II. and the Staff Manual respectively. Title pages will be prepared in manuscript.

O O Ma
19 – 31st

Place	Date	Hour	Summary of Events and Information	Remarks and references to Appendices
Bavilion	19		Nothing of interest	
	20		Visit of Div. commander with of corps ment signed of quartermaster	
	21st		At Bailleul in the offices of divisions	
Le Havre	22nd		Pre arma of marching guard arms arrival for Divisional supply	
	23rd		Took fire on of Hindu and Iron to unload them	
	24th		Divisional Rot Journal and Rot commander for tour	
	25th		So of inference C.D.O.S conv Corps Zelt in Offm for out of year	
	26			
	27		Nothing of interest so of Bailleul last day serve attendant visit Zelt that worse Bailleul in Offm visit of Offm last doss.	
	28			
	29		So Bailleul and Zelt visit units of 9th Brigade	
	30		Journal Division of interest.	
	31		So Bailleul Division Complete and almost now.	

R Allen Capt
D.A.D.O.S
3rd Cav Div

2353 Wt. W2544/1454 700,000 5/15 D. D. & L. A.D.S.S./Forms/C. 2118.

WAR DIARY
or
INTELLIGENCE SUMMARY.

Army Form C. 2118.

S. E. ALLEN Capt
D.A.D.O.S
3rd Cav Div

Place	Date	Hour	Summary of Events and Information	Remarks and references to Appendices
La Hussoye	10.4.15		T.c. in orders dem from 1st & 2nd & 9th Cav Bdes our chief Cont Superior by the A.D.O.S	
	10.8		Went to Gas Cps - A Squn Ordnance matter	
	11.55		2 other vehicles 9c Car exceller Row with up and number of A Bty Ammun Col wondefile by In Cort Letting which together	
	12.9		In Main all Sort	
	1.8		Went to Wilmo and Observe 2nd Bgd Dragoons to A Transport	
	1.11		A D offin officers various various armor	
	1.5		Jun G.R.H.A and Observe fo D Hoar Rifle bPregons in	
			Ops Dept and MSD inn Corporation Polimin front Demande	
	1.11		G.a.a.D.S.S. offices to various a salvae works	
	1.35		Went A Cav Cps for Conference	
			Milieu a report	
	1.9.5		Two Railheads official sound 7th Brigade being only G.D.O.S.	
	2.8.5		Kent Cav Cps & Offices & Comporemen of A.D.O.S.	
	2.35		Railheads had then up all supplies all now come of Calai	

Army Form C. 2118.

WAR DIARY
or
INTELLIGENCE SUMMARY.
(Erase heading not required.)

November 21-30

Place	Date	Hour	Summary of Events and Information	Remarks and references to Appendices
At Havin	22		Went Railhead. Talks with G.S.O.M. and arrangements of Rations.	
	23		G.S. Office and Italia Cavalry Corps. O attree A.D.O.S. Correspondence.	
	24		To office all day as Truck or Railhead.	
	25		Arrived via Three days fast with truck is not sufficient for a Brigade.	
	26		Wire H.Q. 22d Cav Div. I with out trade-mens for A.D.O.S.	
	27		Queued nothing of report.	
	28		To G. Office Railhead and I 2 regiments of An Transport.	
	29		To office all day.	
	30		There all indents at Railhead and cancel some that are required.	

R Allen Capt
D.H.D.O.S
3rd Cav Div

Army Form C. 2118.

WAR DIARY
or
INTELLIGENCE SUMMARY.
(Erase heading not required.)

S.E. ALLEN Capt A.S.C.
DADOS. 3rd Cav Div

December
1 – 31st 1916

Vol 16/17

Place	Date	Hour	Summary of Events and Information	Remarks and references to Appendices
La Hussoie	1-21		Had leave to England from 1st to 21st own to went through affairs during this time via visiting & after can my visit as attended H Q the A.D.O.S. Railhead Montreuil	
	22.		Difficult to get use of car to go Railhead as but issued to write.	
	23.		Writing Q report.	
	24.		Went Railhead.	
	"		Went Railhead opened form of 6 & 8 Brigades another field indent sent out 900 lbs	
	26.		Two issue work at Railhead another indent returned corr. inspection done.	
	27.		Spent day at Railhead checking indents sent out 900 lbs.	
	28.		9.30am – Went over to Railhead	
	29.		Went round units of 7th Brigade checked indent	
	30.		to office all day	
	"		Went Railhead and called to write of 6 & 8 Brigades	

WAR DIARY

S.E. ALLEN Capt
D.A.D.O.S
3rd Cav Div

Army Form C. 2118.

January 1st – 31st 1917

Vol 19

Place	Date	Hour	Summary of Events and Information	Remarks and references to Appendices
Bailly	1st		Nothing to report	
"	2nd		Kit Bailhache Insentment on a Cav Corps	
"	3rd		Somme	
"	4th		Had Quarter master & Tailor	
"	5th		Gunn & Tailness	
Tapires	6th		Lyth Armoured Battery arrived Hotchkiss rifles closed	
	7th		return to report.	
	8-14		I am no Physical Fitness during the period arrived normal	
	17th		The 7th On a time Gun Reraction moved to 1st Canadian Corps	
	19th?		The Information I received Every one attached as Stokes Dennis Gunnery	
	21st?		9. Battn moved to 22d Canadian Division	
	29th		Lyth Armoured Battery issued with 5 Hotchkiss rifles	
	30th			
	31st		Nothing to report. Canadian normal Dennis Training	

S.E. Allen Capt
D.A.D.O.S
3rd Cav Div

D.A.D.O.S.
3RD CAV. DIV'N

Vol 20

Army Form C. 2118.

WAR DIARY
or
INTELLIGENCE SUMMARY.
(Erase heading not required.)

February 1917

Place	Date	Hour	Summary of Events and Information	Remarks and references to Appendices
Tupigny	1–28		During this month the Division has not moved and there has been no special incident. Army Ordnance routine as usual. H. Battery returned to the Division on the 4/2/17 from 2nd Canadian Div. 7th Machine Gun Sqn and Sqn joined from Canadian Corps troops 6/2/17. 8th Machine Gun Sqn from Canadian Division 16/2/17. I have regularly visited units and am continually in touch with the A.O. & D.M.S. and Railhead. Demands for all Fire Arm are normal. From the 20th I have carried out the orders of G.D.O.S. who is on leave and have regularly visited Cavalry Corps H.Q.s. Gunners and daily with all corresponding. Total purchases have been very low indeed.	

J. Allen Capp A.O.D
DADOS
3rd Cav Division

WAR DIARY **S. F. ALLEN**, Capt. Army Form. C. 2118.
or D.A.D.O.S
INTELLIGENCE SUMMARY. 32nd East Div

March 1–31, 1917

Vol 21

Place	Date	Hour	Summary of Events and Information	Remarks and references to Appendices
Tepid	1–31st		During the first of the month I am no longer to report. The balance He was at Marseilles all the time and however I am on leave and only for the 2 upper normal. I am visiting my 20th ordnance, also I am kept informed in fact all Divisional Officers are visited units frequently. I am back in command posts at my troops there all spares & copies and ammo I am connected out and I am back to command. I inspect the army of warehouses I am on command. I am attended the infty conference at the main of the C.D.O.S on garrison attire politically possesses but amounted by last and the H&H then Rifle attachment. I am on complete with the gun carriages, shut must attend some support to that improvement in the ser dept. The Division Co. am completer all the mens of the small box. sprinkler; and R.H hetork I am am withdrawn also to the transport to bar overhauled in Divisional tricken dist.	

R. Allen Capt

Army Form C. 2118.

WAR DIARY
or
INTELLIGENCE SUMMARY.
(Erase heading not required.)

War Diary
April 1st – 30th
1917

S. E. ALLEN Capt AOD
D A D O S
3rd Cav Div

VK 22

Instructions regarding War Diaries and Intelligence Summaries are contained in F.S. Regs., Part II. and the Staff Manual respectively. Title pages will be prepared in manuscript.

Place	Date	Hour	Summary of Events and Information	Remarks and references to Appendices
Inspied	1st		Nil to report	
"	2		Unit Issues along with Pidas	
"	3		Visit BoCR Chiefs Cutter from Blanket's Estaninella	
"	4		Div'sion with order & men their Evacuation Plan from OP.	
MARESQUEL	5		Div'sion moves to Gueusgre Thatras from Mosthure to Beauriainville	
"	6		Visits to the Relieving B'line on complete with Box Trophies and all Otr. fees	
Inontul	7		Div'sion moves to MONCHEL	
Gouy EN ARTOIS	8		Div. Le Gouy EN ARTOIS eastwards Boyemaison with en tte & Ist Pidas	
DOISANS	9		Div'sion moves up to W. of RHES with all units ready Reinste left in action	
"	10		Lemaire's Letter m.o. Pidan Reforments	
"	11		G/Office Fire at Division Appointh Officer W. & Circe	
"	12		Divsion Moves to Fery en Cattre. Large dismounted. % 5th Brigade & 6th Brigade	
"	13		So left div. Emole with Conditioning Option & Lieut-	
"	14		Nil to report	
"	15		11 attention Relin. Homeward 52 het of Gins and Euro. Will them Saddles. amantel	
"	16		& forms refit of 6 & 8 Brigade Pitals. Large amount for Clock Sections S.S.	

Army Form C. 2118.

WAR DIARY
or
INTELLIGENCE SUMMARY.
(Erase heading not required.)

Instructions regarding War Diaries and Intelligence Summaries are contained in F. S. Regs., Part II. and the Staff Manual respectively. Title pages will be prepared in manuscript.

Place	Date	Hour	Summary of Events and Information	Remarks and references to Appendices
WAVANS	16		Dinner given to Wavans	
"	17		Leave demands to L.M & E. Ct Brigades for all Men not units	
"	18		All H.Q. & their Regt. & Vickers On Sect. Officers and H.Q.R.no Cav. holding leaves	
"	19		Dinner given to LIEGESCOURT	
LIEGESCOURT	20		Rested. Beauvoisin Path covering call from Barn	
"	21		Demand All Men visiting units pickets & chickens cast demand	
"	22		Normal	
"	23		At Q Office and Visiting units	
"	24			
"	25		Visiting units northern divisional posts attached Bew supplying coll	
"	26			
"	27		Divising HQ all evening more H.Q.R.no Cav. Rockcliffe up	
"	28		Right of Divisional trains completed 100 out of 205 Saddlery for remount recd.	
"	29		Normal	
"	30		See QQ & G.M.S. Cdre C.D.O.S. demands to units from	

P. Allen Capt. A.o.D.
D.A.D.V.
3rd Cav Div

Army Form C. 2118.

S. E. ALLEN Capt C.O.D.
● DADOS
31st Cav Div

WAR DIARY
or
INTELLIGENCE SUMMARY.
(Erase heading not required.)

May 1st – 31st 1917

Instructions regarding War Diaries and Intelligence Summaries are contained in F. S. Regs., Part II. and the Staff Manual respectively. Title pages will be prepared in manuscript.

Place	Date	Hour	Summary of Events and Information	Remarks and references to Appendices
Suzpicourt	1st		On Saddler up to week following the wire cart.	
"	2nd–9		Dismantle normal but of Office last day as a railhead asking to depart	
"	10th		Dis out of Brestin Hart + Dundy	
"	11th–12th		O! railhead last day leaving Dundy + Dundy ammunition dump	
NAVAS	13th		Division moves to Bastien	
TINCHES	14th		Division moves to Tihner at 6th Div cancelled and Bas changed	
GUÉRRES	15th		Divisional move to GUERRIES to the aerodrome now Bank of Havre the aerodrome	
			Rel to Repts	
HAMELETTE	16th			
	17th		Division moves to Hamelette	
	18th		9th Sapper party recd from work out of the aerodrome	
FLAMICOURT	19th		Division moves to Flamicourt Camp now to Head Quart + the 9 railhead	
	19–31		During the period I have to special duties. The Division was ordered to mobilise + Camping was taken on surveying Cart I flew out all the the aerodrome the to the long from which from work bespoke saw took that upon will report by space cotton (if success working con on a las bourn now it write from south to Perhaps to have to do the Specialty Dept, count from the Depot	

P Allen Capt
6/6/17

Army Form C. 2118.

WAR DIARY
or
INTELLIGENCE SUMMARY.
(Erase heading not required.)

S. E. ALLEN Capt.
A.O.D
DADOS
3rd Cav Div

June 1 – 31/07
1917

Place	Date	Hour	Summary of Events and Information	Remarks and references to Appendices
Hamisorit			During the mth. B Sqn mostly three ZG. Gun cushing	

During the mth I record this ran Gun coming up by detachm
of MG. Bran. Any Officer and dumps are also together
as all Bicycle H. quarter an apparently clean &
made them I assess from of their MG direct from dump
The ammunition MG ZG Gun Vehicles are kept
very oft oftn spare pts. I have kept a record of 1000
S.B. Vehicles in accordance with Army Instruction and
issued a C.H especially of Sa. I contain Officer and man
also holding a reserve of 1250 of their. With Cav. Regt
from another aBn. Vehicles are also in Cav. to X.H.S.
an some units force is difficult of moves them when
they are beyond mtr. B no horse teams a span call
cart of this offn. affically could in overcomn. I have
hept in touch with my G. Officer and the A.D.O.S all
local front Holters Gn the mostly ZG. Gun hept in communication.

(A7092). Wt. W12839/M1293. 75,000. 1/17. D.D. & L., Ltd. Forms/C.2118/4.

Army Form C. 2118.

WAR DIARY
or
INTELLIGENCE SUMMARY.
(Erase heading not required.)

Place	Date	Hour	Summary of Events and Information	Remarks and references to Appendices
FLAMICOURT			All ammunition has been previously have been too little. Front trenches are 2000 mus per Division and can now fire "buman" who then firen on 6 three guns as a ammunition that are out this total. Taken off	

G.G - 9 M.S.
3rd Cav Div

Attached is my "War Diary" for
July, 1917. Please.

R Allen Capt
D A D O S
13/8/17   3rd Cav Div

TB 15/8

WAR DIARY
or
INTELLIGENCE SUMMARY.

Army Form C. 2118.

S. E. ALLEN Capt. A.G.O.B.
D.A.D.O.S
3rd Cavalry Division

July 1st–31st 1917

Place	Date	Hour	Summary of Events and Information	Remarks and references to Appendices
FLAMICOURT	1st–3rd		This country by itself does not offer any thing of any particular interest. One of the Reg. of H.T. The Armoured to F.H.Q. is troops here and work in unloading ammunition in continuation of a order.	
TREUX	4th		Division moved from FLAMICOURT to TREUX and at 10th Aug and the candles kept here from to write out up 24th June the morning and 2 lane of sufficient breadth there for carrying .	
DOULLENS	5th		Div HQ. arrives at Authieu & report Division moves to Doullens	
FRAMECOURT BERNES	6th 7th 7th 16th		Division moves to Framecourt Div HQ. at Berves and Havrier arrive at Bernay, with relieved Div demand to meet with 2 men and 3 cars & wire from my here and anten. Brew then from Havre & Calais and Chan & have another that & Havre, thick Adams arrived & here now thin are the only Div Staff with Expense.	
BOSNES	16th 2nd 3rd		Division moves to Bosnes 2 with each cars on a way chances at the Depp Here as supplying out that studs 152 and from the past Div and coming up . I cannot get sufficient MSP because no Battery is available but have demanded more int Dr Offi support. I after a G.D.O.S Army for three of the G.D.O-S a train. Then the form officially is obtaining the of out our Dur Dum that to Div Army up from Base but the 6 not only marked. Then to Div a motion of medium type return want but the 10 non Bre cancels out all Division Per Unit Here was then Bre form.	

R. Allen Capt.
D.A.D.O.S
3rd Cav. Div.

WAR DIARY

S.E. ALLEN Capt
A.D.M.S.
D A D O S
3rd Cav Division

August 1917

Place	Date	Hour	Summary of Events and Information	Remarks and references to Appendices
Bussus	1 – 31		During the month I have no special action to record. The various F.A. Inns at Cav during the past month are in a good working order and I inform D upstairs necessary that I have no heavy demands. Duro at from Base have shown our trans as at week are well up in all time. Owing to shortage of accommodation I have been for APM & DAPM in Common HQs at Bar Sur sur Noye and I suggest the moment that I demand that the persons I am of opinion that units could the further when their normal demands are as I think we I am sending G.S. computation Statement at the end of last month. I there wish in order to emit. The A.G + G.M.S check a MS I am to write.	

R Allen Capt
DADOS
3rd Cav Div

62/9

A.A.G of M.S.
3rd Cav Div

My War Diary for September (91)
ant herewith.

R Allen Capt
DA DQS

7/10/19

WAR DIARY

Army Form C. 2118.

War Diary / INTELLIGENCE SUMMARY
(Erase heading not required)

September 1st to 31st 1917

S.E. ALLEN Capt.
A.O.D.
DADOS
31st Cavalry Division

Vol 27

Place	Date	Hour	Summary of Events and Information	Remarks and references to Appendices
BOSNES	1-31st		During this month I can no fully of importance. The Division has not moved or reached and my Dumps have not changed. Both the Receptions of ORDN Clothing, Khit have not been coming up all from our own Inf. very weak and worn out our Inf. There has been an increase in the issue of fast worn clothing. During the month I have visited at I unit with a view to reducing demands for clothing Sec and the system of drawing week from this Forts by companies with this units in them demand. ten food for that & made for full win Rations. It is now our home L that the Companies note a in accordance with forma. I am hept in close touch with the office of Dir. Sec. I day and visited all unit fw month. The system of smally belt demands on Bow of D.R.L.S. works to give the present satisfaction.	

S.E. Allen Capt
DADOS
31st Cav Div

DADOS 3 Army Form C. 2118.

S.E. ALLEN Capt. A.O.D
DADOS
3rd Cav D" **WAR DIARY**
or
INTELLIGENCE SUMMARY.
Month 1917

(Erase heading not required.)

Army Form C. 2118.

Place	Date	Hour	Summary of Events and Information	Remarks and references to Appendices
Blendecques	1st		Divisional Head Quarters at Blendecques AIRE the amount	
			was quite normal to no specific hour to turn plant was	
			the 1st to 16th. 3 horses die March into summary	
Blendecques	17th		Divisional summary of PERNES railhead that our army at AIRE	
Aire-Houdain	22nd		Divisional summary from PERNES to HOUDAIN-HOUIGNUIL	
DOMART	23rd		from & DOMART-EN-PONTHIEU railhead CANDAS	
	24th		I went off to have and what the end of south railway line	
			The enemy attacked and were checked. During the scrap	
			all limbers lost came up with love from the S Bde Trench Mor	
			Bar and filled with Q C Collars from each and 3rd Bkdes	
			I am very proud that I took Div. in HQ the 3rd Div	
			surrounded fellows & that my unit only ordinary losses I am	
			very pleased.	
			D. Allen Capt	

WAR DIARY
or
INTELLIGENCE SUMMARY
(Erase heading not required)

Army Form C. 2118.

S.E. ALLEN Capt
A.D.O.S.
D.A.D.O.S.
3rd Cav Div

NOVEMBER 1-30 1916

Place	Date	Hour	Summary of Events and Information	Remarks and references to Appendices
DOMART EN PONTIEU	1-16		During this period my Office and Stores were at Domart and Pailliart at Candas. Brigades were occasionally Billeted and this Div. in H.I. We were at rest and Clothing and Equipment was carried in bulk. Much kit walked to a complete state in view with Brilliant results. I inspected my issues of kit from Field and also that I & S required for Divisions &c The Divisional H.Q.Bttn after we parade on 2 Nov and our Rebel Btns were at work & officer & casualties.	
SUZANNE	17-23		Driver Van Trouten & Dvr. Bate L. arriving but I had no issue except this entire for R. Watts to Decamp the Hackling & I these that we were after ordered. Railhead Police Gave my Clerks and Office in Beauquesne and Lodge occupancy Billets were then the Command not heavy and all up the Ntl 9 men. During this mth. I visited the Cavan'n. Div. Bn Can wkg and am Sheller at	
BEAUQUESNE	23-29		Railhead Para and also Div Stores. All three after ham also Div issues.	
	30		My clerks and Office at Calin. November Rly Returns only Stores will Hitherto Bttn appearance in Corrns. Mo. during month on better than.	

R. Allen Capt
DADOS 3rd Cav Div

Army Form C. 2118.

S.E. ALLEN Capt
A.P.D.
DAPO7
3rd Cavalry Division

WAR DIARY
INTELLIGENCE SUMMARY

December 1-31 1917

Place	Date	Hour	Summary of Events and Information	Remarks and references to Appendices
CORBIE	1st 20th		Had an order to Divisions and Bde Troops at Corbie. The Comeress Troops remain from are a known where Troops in station. Demand came in of hy2 and other chitties of part of station. Demand an onset of unit now and rest Divel work of old left Divin Alliance of unit now and in removed on The First Division left Divis - Comd and I removed on known of 5 to the station to Domart for Divis on hour for the own to very time & bit within peach down & difficulty appointment in Albumeny rather from Bar. The At 8 pm Tegh an element car arrived from Bar. Then	
DOMART FN POIX HILL	21st		Divisioin and to Domart - Roothses & Bendes with draw from from my Journey to Domart and other than 4 pm to be Checked. Demand for the candidates of advance again. team number of unit next and Act Divisions and Divisions Commander Post and from a few Dep or run from Ben an for Commander in the both and suffered in Sheamer had from Ben To held up as K Reading was numerous in Mr first up for L.D.D. Told chops - I Thomson all offr about to take 0) remarks I have called for admen and to Commanders in Amorew Mr write up offn Pince B, with weta and offn of officer are after the such offn full of your under the until up weak remarks	

J. Allen Capt

Army Form C. 2118.

WAR DIARY
or
INTELLIGENCE SUMMARY

(Erase heading not required.)

R Allen Capt
A.O.O.D
D.A.D of
3rd Cav Division

January 1–31
1916

Vol 31

Instructions regarding War Diaries and Intelligence Summaries are contained in F. S. Regs., Part II. and the Staff Manual respectively. Title pages will be prepared in manuscript.

Place	Date	Hour	Summary of Events and Information	Remarks and references to Appendices
DOMART EN PONTHIEU	1st 2nd 3rd		During the march of the 3rd Division in the zone not occupied by other GS staff men allotted with the reception of Horse S.D. and S.A.A. incidental to accident I took this up & the personnel Division was sent on to Domart and Belloise at Gorda and Vieil Arries then Van from Domart to Van Transport. I & Horses all met after Van A.S.C unit that was filled all out off, and extensive damage after arrival in Garrison till Var office without act off in regiment. During the march this was to think fit for barracks dept sent out & transports arrived. During this period 2nd & 3rd Cavalry Bdes belonging to C.D.S then were on their 3 nights in about 2 Coll of my officers had quarters at 3rd Cav Div the time and 150 men of the 2nd Coll for miners & as and were Boarded. Indicated after return to D.D.O.S 2nd M Domart. The formation of E.O.Q Forces. The 3rd Cav Div march & forward on the 30th/1/16 the changing over of the 5th Cav Div Corps in charge to occur. This on interior Survey	
AMIENS & INGERSHEIM			R Allen Capt A.O.O.D 3rd Cav Div	

A891.   Wt. W1422/M1160 350,000 12/16   D. D. & L.   Forms/C./2118/14.

Army Form C. 2118.

WAR DIARY
or
INTELLIGENCE SUMMARY
(Erase heading not required.)

F. Allen Capt
A.D.D.
2nd Can Div

February 1-28 1916

Place	Date	Hour	Summary of Events and Information	Remarks and references to Appendices
Moncheaux Festu	1-10		Throughout this period the Division has been at rest in the railroad at La Chapelette for church parades. The railroad at La Chapelette for church services was quite inadequate and as the men have been received into churches there was a church in a church in the area of news. The Canadians & Army Service Corps have had their own kits, bags and both have duly received their services. But it could be a big advantage to the Canadians and allies established for a Divisional Canadian Svc. & the critical as I refer to to all therules and means that the reserve in 14th in use of in plenty of carrying there is at present had scarcer absence in Jan 3 division at rest a rest centre. Every of list of week having was not an altar work and the quarterback during part of the journey of H.T. sent entails extra handling all my [illegible] and with the CS2 and applicable he & so much of some & extra before there is a advice for an unit to [illegible] and this ensure to allowing movement and the platform crew all to leave by application for all the [illegible] and 2nd ACB or Communion service, during my absence there is no entry & never.	
	10-28			

F. Allen Capt.

WAR DIARY
or
INTELLIGENCE SUMMARY

Army Form C. 2118.

S.E. ALLEN Capt
DADOS
3rd Cavalry Division

Vol 33

March 1–31st 1918

Place	Date	Hour	Summary of Events and Information	Remarks and references to Appendices
Inchy & Catelet	1–13		Divisional Head Quarters at Inchy & later Ell 13th 2a.ahoot at BRIE and later at La Chappelette. My Office and Dumps also Ammunition MSP and Pontoon Mule MSP one at Inchy and one at La Chapelette all up to Ordnance MSP one Part & my dumps for my disposition as a check against unit demands. Routhead still at La Chapelette, demand for Pistol arms & Ammunition MSP and Pontoon Mule MSP, kept both occupied and returned demands to Base.	
ATHIES	18th–21st		Division arrived and the three ornate Allotted & DADOS Indian mess allotment quite inadequate and quartered in Pon. Buy trial of money allies.	
VARESNES	22nd			
Catelet	23rd		During this period ASR-Rln, PnP, Pickan M Gun Rifle Oil and MGpa Grease both them also Belts & Bulb Bow Urban was the MSP most in demand. Gun Park was at LONGEAU and consequently a long way off. Getting and all Stes MSP was issued thus possible. But Parts was not Ammunn- Upload, I was able to repair Hotchkin Riffes in the	
Chingy-au-Bort	26th			
to Crand / Dan	27th			
NO SUPPLY	28th		Armoured MSP and was able to meet all demands for arms & Sundries & LONGEAU but the distance caused some delay. I suggest that during similar future operation a Bn & More Stes Carts will adv or DSP is issued on list & Divisional Loan is addition & Stes searcher Cpm.	

Allen Capt

S.E. ALLEN Capt Army Form C. 2118.
DADOS
3rd Cav Div

WAR DIARY
or
INTELLIGENCE SUMMARY.
(Erase heading not required.)

April 1st to 30th 1918

Instructions regarding War Diaries and Intelligence Summaries are contained in F. S. Regs., Part II. and the Staff Manual respectively. Title pages will be prepared in manuscript.

Place	Date	Hour	Summary of Events and Information	Remarks and references to Appendices
RIVERY	1st to 11th		Am dump &c at Pont de Metz and Railhead Amiens. During this time demands were heavy because Division was refitting. Great difficulty experienced with 4 Bat.s of M.G. especially have been not armed but eventually arrival of M.G's became regular.	
Lonne & Rolion	12		Division move to Lonne & Rolion.	
Rolion	13		To Ypres and my dump Office and Railhead also Div H.Q. we all at Rolion and at refitting continued. The R.H.A Battery joined the Division on the 12th but as its cordork not received ther could only arrive fire after Zeller Art Office approval. I have been no cables taken to replace 2 complete 07.15 Bn. that about 2 wks previous on 5.00 p.m. ammunition complete. All this coming up will except known this & Stores also horse from Stores have also been Horse.	

Allen Capt

Army Form C. 2118.

WAR DIARY
or
INTELLIGENCE SUMMARY.
(Erase heading not required.)

A.D.Vick Conductor - Captain
DADOS Law Div
Vol. 35

Place	Date	Hour	Summary of Events and Information	Remarks and references to Appendices
PERNES	1st to 4th		Dump, Office & Railhead. The process of refitting the Division was here completed. Stores arrived regularly from Base and demands ceased to be so heavy. The return of Winter Clothing was carried on and the Pinth evacuated. The placing of two Boxes of Horse Shoes on each lorry of the Supply Column was commenced and later completed; this enabled a standard reserve to be maintained.	
WAIL	5/5/18		Dump and Office.	
YVRENCH	6/5/18		Dump and Office. Railhead - DOMART-ST-LEGER. Division was supplied with miscellaneous stores while on the move.	
CONTAY	6/5/18 to 14/5/18		Office was here with Divisional Head Qrs Dump at DOMART-ST-LEGER. Anti Gas appliances handed over to D.G. Officer. During this month 33 Hotchkin Guns were issued to the Division	
YZEUX	14/5/18 To 31/5/18		15 of which were instructional and 18 were to replace those with Pistol Grip. In Divisional Armourers Shop 24 Hotchkin Guns were repaired also 4 Vickers Guns 14 Bicycles and 144 Rifles. Office at YZEUX Dump at DOMART-ST-LEGER.	W.Vickers Conductor W. Captain DADOS (Front on LEAVE)

WAR DIARY
or
INTELLIGENCE SUMMARY.

Army Form C. 2118.

S.E. ALLEN
DADVS
3rd Cav Div

June 1st–31st 1918

WD 3 Appendices

Place	Date	Hour	Summary of Events and Information	Remarks and references to Appendices
1–31			The Division Hd. Qurs. in not very new Qur. posn and 3 from Qur. area, a special team till the 27th. The Division Vet: officer prior to my departure after consultation with Principal Vety Officer my absence and up to the once of the arrival of Major ac- Qurn adviser the unit effective and routine of all Vet. held at his memorial at Potagen are booksaid mail pouch at Yzeux.	

A. Allen Maj
DDVS

WAR DIARY July 1918

INTELLIGENCE SUMMARY.

SEALLEN Maj
G.O.D
DADo's
32nd Cavalry Division

Vol 37

Army Form C. 2118.

Place	Date	Hour	Summary of Events and Information	Remarks and references to Appendices
YZEUX			During the T.A.O. of the month Div. H.Q. have been at YZEUX and Railhead at ST LEGER LE DOMART up till 20/7/18 then at CANDAS & HANGEST. I have no special to say I regret the shifting has not been other. I cannot but view I regret movements have not been heavy. There have been abnormal repairs from Bde. on & Divy. Recce been no complaints. The Garrisons Mgs. Sec. Div. & Div. to Brigades and has full support. The Passages & spans & roads over the river kept Bdes. Artly Gorrisons with clear shot and clear Rifle. With & Cut off and as it too lane door Shot Cavalry mounted have those with the pieces to always be ridden when the arm pasts. The Mk. 28 Truck in a later arm and he on Pst at Ft but off & Infantry on in Sum hides. Been issued & Rollers and are work fixed. We & little been in used & spleen. Bat Expr. the D.G.O. m.p. when the Bn— respiration and trophele all off. Whenever. As W. from on whenever to on and a Chief Grenoble on a riots & ammo chain issue.

Rollo Maj
DDDos

WAR DIARY
or
INTELLIGENCE SUMMARY.

Army Form C. 2118.

S. E. ALLEN Major
A.O.D
D.A.D.O.S
3rd Cav Division

August 1918

Place	Date	Hour	Summary of Events and Information	Remarks and references to Appendices
YZEUX	1/8/18	15"	Divisional H.Q at YZEUX and Railhead at HANGEST. the Division is up to date with ordnance stores all Divisional MOPs are received at my ord the 3rd Divl am French D.S. Fill Armistice are attended to unit. The Armourers WKSP is still kept all employed and a Armature WKSP will be attached to me or the Province come from Base. I am holding down Base in Antwerpoefies. I am holding down WKS in Antwerpoefies. I am holding down WKS in Antwerpoefies of operations and a 6th a 3rd 24th plan my two cars up to Ford Loaded with an enstallment of Min. Shells 2nd required and for Loadies all to immediately and remain at Railhead ready 2 man Guard and siren on top a Shells/or allows, Lio Lorro oil to Kept empty & also Guns.	
PONT A MET	6/8/18		Went to PONT A METZ Railhead Salvere Lorres KKr. WKhs but I am all righted. Went from my Lorres also Sone could WKhs also proceeds to Bontoolery.	
BOIS a BARBS	8/8/18		Division 24 Rev went to Sporalecom 2 Co. WKt a and my Officer and Dumb semain at Railhead 3 Lorries 9 for tracer WKt me to most immediate demand in all this the situation now setting it recreance the Lorries & come forward to the ...	
			when Shells are made to & went from them down WKh me one of Ords Lorres on a D car & troops in Bus 2 will work throughout and must often report Supports. I found that HOPKins Cartsaddeling in required during Specialison were on a own H.R is opened & it is usually useless & issue a issue & an WKDSP, Cavallore & run down Saturday up. My Goom of Vukan Bolts are not required are during the advance and it are all to fit up Gollar Collect. By Supports that this required not 2 a Limon at Railhead "HANGE" the Adjut & Douart the Hampl after Division Train Refilled Ord equipment must sam WKs in private Specialism. Should have a Train Sam 24/8/18 the Division Lorres are refilled.	
YZEUX	15/8/18			

Allen Maj.

WAR DIARY or INTELLIGENCE SUMMARY

September 1918

S.F. Allen C.O.D. 2nd Army Form C. 2118.
3rd Cav Div.

Hour, Date, Place	Summary of Events and Information	Remarks and references to Appendices
Fontaine l'Abbé 6/9/18	Returned from leave 6/9/18. Railhead at Frévent. The demands are now kept out covering from Bois ... etc. Ammunition Supp + Troops the Supply kept our outposts and I feel more of note in case of move or transfer of Base.	
Maroeuil 26/9/18	Division moves + railhead moves to Plateau. No more allowed and not capable of carrying the amount known as cost capacity of the B. Proportion etc and also the ammunition Supp and supplies for 3 ton lorries on horses that must be authorized and known that time the movement Supp must be covered give up 4 lorries there is provision for the lorries are available + clear back + carry	
Etrun 27.9.18		
Gouvieux 30.9.18	Per Third units are available 2 lath supply moving. Give 3 tan + two on Peltan. Ammunition Supp + Prov Belt in Base 1 lorry, can be Rot 1 lorry. Home from 1 lorry. From a new Supp omni hit + other resv. 1 lorry. 5000 both field ammo Supplies Oil etc 1 lorry, + the lorry. 30 cwt lorry ammo ... this Supply last troops to form a new this Supply or a more ...	Allen Maj

WAR DIARY or INTELLIGENCE SUMMARY

Army Form C. 2118.

S.E. Allen Major
3rd Cav. Bde. Divi'n

Month October 1916

Place	Date	Hour	Summary of Events and Information	Remarks and references to Appendices
GOEUVILLY	1/10/16		Battalion Relieved but changed to Thousand Reserve 11/10/16 normal week more to work.	V.D.4.0
MARETZ	10/10/16		Railroad Thousand Reserve within 6 & Oct back in Reserve. Gas Men & Baths issued round all the troops up and from Ron.	
Clari	11/10/16		Been Regiment area & Piccard were kept accumulating of fish at our dumps.	
Bethin	12/10/16			
Hunnin Lost Offspt	13/10/16		Gas Ban issued Railhead change to Le Translong and a half common during the rest of the month. There is nothing of importance to report except that the demand on heavy foot esp. round from Bar and which Limit. The 200 Black horses from to Flands up to the 10th Lust split without help less apparent to onboard into the Holland as S.S. bajon and an Infantry Lastern.	

Allen Major
15/11/16

Army Form C. 2118.

WAR DIARY
or
INTELLIGENCE SUMMARY.
(Erase heading not required.)

November 1916

S.F. Allen Major
R A O C
DADOS
3rd Cavalry Division

Instructions regarding War Diaries and Intelligence Summaries are contained in F. S. Regs., Part II. and the Staff Manual respectively. Title pages will be prepared in manuscript.

Place	Date	Hour	Summary of Events and Information	Remarks and references to Appendices
Hanan ?	1/11/16		I still have a large accumulation of the washing dirty & duplicates of linen from Bar and Laundry and in anticipation of a move I am evacuating 6 mnt & Bar & D. Car.	
Saint ?	7/11/16		Have different mor and various para also sheds & most important elements on the march. I consider that sheds are worth a most important lorry.	
Ham	12/11/16		Railhead closed at 6 Truck arriv 3am arr 4 men rain.	
Bastelli	13/11/16		Qnd Q report	
Pozieres	15/11/16		Railhead 30 Kilos distant half my lorries in Wspn. have I seen the dumps one at H.Q. one at Railhead but am issuing rations. Must unit an draw in from dumps.	
Bethune	21/11/16		Qnd Q report	
Peronne	27/11/16		I want now 13 Car A.H.B.S. at Pozieres and drew rations for them - the Bottom or for from run Posts. It is laid down that Battalions are responsible for the evacuation of unserviceable items and of spare mules to Ordnance Officer. This done; but as Posts are distant and so are also the Car heavy after I submit that Battalions as division cannot easily draw from Post and that there is time to kept up & railhead the same mules to kept up & railhead.	

Walter Mor

27.8.08.

WAR DIARY
or
INTELLIGENCE SUMMARY

3rd Cavalry Divn Army Form C. 2118.

December 1918.

(Erase heading not required.)

Place	Hour, Date	Summary of Events and Information	Remarks and references to Appendices
PERWEZ.	9/12/18	Office & Dump Maintained at NAMUR. Large quantities of stores being received for Divisions have formed a railhead dump. Am issuing from here in some cases. Several cases of necessary repairs to horses but stores supplied regularly to Units. Demands for 3rd Hundred submitted to Base.	
SOHEIT TINLOT	16/12/18	(Office) Arrived at this village & Dump at HUY. Railhead then for 15th the following day 16/19. Railhead moved to SERAINE. Supplied by road men to Units and several men on leave, these soldiers moved extra work for remainder	
	30/12/18	Railhead moves to ENGIS. Stores issued regularly -	

WAR DIARY
or
INTELLIGENCE SUMMARY
(Erase heading not required.)

Army Form C. 2118.

Place	Date	Summary of Events and Information	Remarks and references to Appendices
SOHEIT TINLOT	23/7/18	BASTS (Major S.E. Allen) leaves Division for England. New BASTS (Major H. Smith) granted leave to U.K. before joining the Division.	
NANDRIN	29/7/18	Office moves to NANDRIN. Next dump for over a week. During which of the work Shoemakers shops employed - many repairs carried out.	[signature] Major BASTS 3rd Cav Div'n.

Army Form C. 2118.

DADOS 3 Cav R

WAR DIARY or INTELLIGENCE SUMMARY

(Erase heading not required.)

Instructions regarding War Diaries and Intelligence Summaries are contained in F. S. Regs., Part II. and the Staff Manual respectively. Title pages will be prepared in manuscript.

Place	Date	Hour	Summary of Events and Information	Remarks and references to Appendices
NANDRIN	1/31/1/19		During the month visited several Units in the Division & inspected 2nd line stores. I found same quite satisfactory. The following additional Units have been posted to me for administration. E.H.R. Physical Tr. School. Armrd. (Cycling) Camp. 50 C.C.S. 724 Labour Coy & No. 14 ADM. Stores. The following Unit left the Divn. 221 A.T.R.S. Coy. Very small demands recd. for Detail Stores, but the BULK demands still very heavy. A.B.R.O. has been published calling attention to this which no doubt will show an improvement next month. A few complaints received in regard to supply of trucks, but this was through a large number having been still in route from Base, stores being depleted in Open trucks and simply disappearing covering the stores. I have reported the matter to Col. Calais & suggested if stores had to be conveyed in open trucks a covering man should be sent with same. I have received no reply to my letter, yet it was again though too promised to take up the matter.	
	10/1/19		Major H. SMITH R.A.O.C. joined as DADOS in place of Major SE. ALLEN to England.	Authy. A.G. Letter No. AG/504/3(b) + HQ. Third Army C/4450 d/22/12/18.
	19/1/19		Visited Major Brooks OC Released P.W. Camp Liège in regard to taking over Ordnance & Red Cross stores on account of the Camp closing down. A lorry load of stores dumped at Residence & Liège sent to 7 Stopant. Consignation. B. Ordnance stores returned by me — Red Cross stores handed over to 50 C.C.S. HUY.	

Signed Major
DADOS 3rd Cav Divn

Army Form C. 2118.

WAR DIARY
INTELLIGENCE SUMMARY
(Erase heading not required.)

Instructions regarding War Diaries and Intelligence Summaries are contained in F.S. Regs., Part II. and the Staff Manual respectively. Title pages will be prepared in manuscript.

Date, Place	Summary of Events and Information	Remarks and references to Appendices
1/2/19. NANDRIN	During the whole of the month stores arrived regularly from the Base & rejoices moved to Units. In many instances trucks on arriving at Nandrin were found to have fallen open & contents pilfered, especially such items as boots, soap. I have reported the matter to A.D.O.S. suggesting a new class be used for carrying the stores from the Base. Store tents & enclosures have been demanded from Base & received in anticipation of Units becoming demobilisation. Any present store sheds at ENGIS are quite suitable for an Intermediate Collecting Station. Big issues have been made of shelters for the Z Horse depot SERAINGS & Animal Collecting Camp. ENGIS. Camp Kettles & harness lamps demanded & issued to O.C. Animal Collecting Camp for conducting parties proceeding overland from the Base.	
3/2/19. NANDRIN	Proceeded to NAMUR. D.D.O.S. Found Army & representing A.D.V.S. busy — Corps at a Conference on Demobilization —	
4/2/19. — " —	Visited A.D.V.S. Corps at SPA and gave him a detailed account of what had taken place at the Conference the previous day.	
10/2/19 — " —	Moved my Office to ENGIS.	

Army Form C. 2118.

WAR DIARY
INTELLIGENCE SUMMARY
(Erase heading not required.)

Hour, Date, Place	Summary of Events and Information	Remarks and references to Appendices
ENGIS 9/7/19	3rd Dragoon Guards returned stores surplus to their strength.	
10/7/19	7th ditto — ditto — ditto —	
12/7/19	Remaining Units returned their surplus stores.	
13/7/19	3rd R.H.Q. & 7th Bde. H.Q. N/72 D.A.C. C & R Batteries N/L returned their bicycles, watches, binoculars & prismatic compasses (except Title N/Base 12 subsection (11) Army Remount Depot, Calais, France.	
27/7/19	Informed that the Canadian Brigade was leaving the Division on the 2nd August 1919. Cancelled all outstanding indents & informed respective Units — moved Units of the Brigade to Cav. Corps Troops for administration. During the month the undermentioned Units have been posted from us for administration:— 57th a.t. Coy R.E. 110 Labour Coy. & 169 P.O. War Coy. The following Units have left the Division:— G.H.Q. Physical Training & 110 Labour Coy.	

Ernest Mayo
Brass
3rd Cav. Div.

www.ingramcontent.com/pod-product-compliance
Lightning Source LLC
Chambersburg PA
CBHW081549160426
43191CB00011B/1876